DAWN O'PORTER lives in Los Angeles with her husband Chris, her two boys Art and Valentine, and her cat Lilu and dog Potato. Dawn started out in TV production but quickly landed in front of the camera, making numerous documentaries for the BBC and Channel 4, the most famous being her immersive investigations of polygamy, size zero, childbirth, free love, breast cancer and the movie *Dirty Dancing*.

Dawn is now a full-time, *Sunday Times* bestselling author of seven books who, at the time of writing, never leaves the house.

www.dawnoporter.co.uk
@hotpatooties
/DawnOPorter

Also by Dawn O'Porter

FICTION

The Cows

So Lucky

DAWN O'PORTER

HarperCollins*Publishers*

HarperCollins*Publishers* Ltd
1 London Bridge Street,
London SE1 9GF

www.harpercollins.co.uk

First published by HarperCollins*Publishers* 2020
4

A catalogue record for this book is available from the British Library

ISBN: 978-0-00-843187-7 (HB)
ISBN: 978-0-00-843188-4 (TPB)

Set in Berling LT Std by Palimpsest Book Production Ltd,
Falkirk, Stirlingshire

Printed and bound in the UK by CPI Group (UK) Ltd,
Croydon CR0 4YY

This book is produced from independently certified FSC™ paper to ensure
responsible forest management.

For more information visit: www.harpercollins.co.uk/green

Dedicated to all my family and friends who I miss so much.
Soon, we shall dance again.

What a shitshow of a year.

Contents

Introduction

Dear 2020,

Earlier this year I got myself a paper diary. I wanted to go back to writing things down, rather than having everything on my phone. I found it today and got so sad when I saw how empty it was. Just months of nothing. No people, no meetings, no life. I sat and looked at it and got a little weepy. There was supposed to be all this other stuff, and it just wasn't there. There was only emptiness.

As always, in January, I started the year with great intentions and felt good about what was heading my way. I wanted a better balance of deadlines and parenting. We'd just returned from Christmas in Ireland and, while the rest of the world dieted, I continued to eat like my life depended on it until my forty-first birthday on 23 January (feel free to write that down). It's always my most greedy month, because as soon as New Year is done, I get into birthday mode. I celebrate a lot every year. Multiple dinners and events, I've always been the same. Delighted to reach another age, excited to be healthy and (generally) happy. My birthday passed and I remained committed to making small improvements to my life – none of which involved more exercise, less food or smaller measures of tequila, but I had deleted Instagram from my phone (lasted a week). I'd started to search for a therapist to iron out the many creases that form by the time you hit your forties.

All in all, I was ready to continue to ride through this decade with a margarita in one hand and novels spouting from the fingers of the other. As Chris and I rose from the swamp of having babies we wanted to party more, dance more, write more and fuck more. Everything was on track for life to become really fun. I'd waft drunkenly through my forties, hosting parties in our garden, wearing vibrant kaftans, living off tequila and weed gummies. That was how it was going to be. Until that one Saturday morning when I woke up and everything went dark.

My friend Caroline Flack took her own life on 15 February. She was my funniest friend. It broke me. I remain unfixed. One of the worst things I could imagine happening had happened. All plans stopped. My forties were off.

This isn't a book about Caroline, what happened to her or why. But to understand my emotional experiences of lockdown, you need to know how it began. I was grieving, and in a pretty terrible way. I quit Twitter. I refused to read the tabloids, or even listen to negativity. I wanted to be alone. I wanted to isolate (careful what you wish for). I wanted my life to be smaller (not that small, thanks Covid-19). Something seismic had happened to me and a lot of the people I love. The world could never be the same again, and then suddenly, it wasn't. During that weird space of time between losing Caroline and isolation kicking in, I felt like I was in a world full of people who would never understand me again. Most of my friends were in London, my husband, Chris, and I were in LA in our own sad and cloudy bubble. I felt a million miles from home, but was also terrified of returning to London for the emotional memories it would throw at me. Caroline is embedded into those streets, how could I ever walk down them without screaming?

As the world started to change it felt like it was all connected. When I flew back to Los Angeles from London after the funeral the borders were literally closing behind me. I was surrounded by people in masks. The air was full of anxiety, like a huge volcano had erupted and the lava was heading towards us, no one having any idea when it would stop. For the first few days after I got home, I found it a struggle to get through reading a story to my kids. A week later, my cat pissed all over the sofa and I couldn't smell it. Food didn't taste of anything. I put the rough throat down to having cried my way through the previous week, but as I waved coffee under my nose and got nothing, the news broke that losing your sense of smell was a symptom. Other friends that I had been with in London started to get ill. For them it was fever, flu, days and days in bed. By all accounts, I was lucky. We all wondered if it was coronavirus itself but didn't really believe it. Still sort of joking about it, questioning all the ridiculous hype. We had no way to find out. There were no tests at that point. Only the realisation that the global pandemic was striking us all, and the people in charge hadn't done anything to protect us. Oh God, I thought to myself as the schools closed and the restaurants locked their doors, we're all totally fucked.

What you are about to read are highlights from the (almost) daily diary I wrote from the start of isolation until the summer of 2020 when we moved house. I went from being a working mother with high demands and deadlines to suddenly being a full-time stay-at-home mum. I tackled this with varying levels of success. I had to step up my mum game, protect my kids from my grief, be emotionally available for my husband and basically pull my shit together way sooner than I think was right. Be prepared for a lot of parenting, drinking, edibles, shitting, pissing (the kids and the cat, not me), crying and analysing. But amid the stresses, there was a lot of good too. When life was stripped right back to the bones, I realised how strong my skeleton was. I have changed a lot since 15 February, and I'm happy to share the process and thoughts that go with it.

2020 is the year that changed us all, and maybe that is OK.

Love Dawn x

PIECE ONE

Full-Time Stay-at-Home Mum

18 March
Isolation Update – Totally holding it together

Well there goes another day of total bollocks. Look, I plan to get my shit together and storm through this with grace, but I need a week of being an asshole first. They are saying the schools will be closed here until September? Whoa. I presume by then we will have tests, so we can at least share the kids with other 'negative' families, and get them some playdates going? We're not dealing with the bubonic plague here. I get that we need to stop it spreading, but it can't fill us all with so much fear that we never leave the house again . . . can it? I just want to get these two weeks of isolation over, so I can drop my kids off at their friends' houses occasionally – that would make all the difference. I'm not sure what the deal with having any childcare is, because how can I control what that person does with their time while they are not with us? Kid share sounds more likely. With families who you know are doing everything right.

MY GOD THIS IS MENTAL.

It's blowing my mind to think that just last week I was with a friend in London. We said goodbye to my sweet Caroline and among the sadness of it all, I was making jokes about coronavirus, saying how I wouldn't have risked getting it for anyone else. Not so funny now.

I woke up with a cold and have felt low energy and a bit glum all day. Although I did do an hour of 'school' with my son Art. This involved teaching him how to write the letter N, and finding things around the house, and in his books, beginning with N. We both got bored, but he can now spell 'Nope', so it wasn't an entire waste of time.

I forgot to give the kids lunch then, when I remembered, they ate it like it was their first meal in years.

I'm eating too many crisps. Today I had them with a mayonnaise-based dip. I plan to do that most days. If I'm going down, I want to do it slathered in mayonnaise, eating Kettle Chips. Is that too much to bloody ask?

Talking of going down, I have had Dido's 'White Flag' stuck in my head for days. Nice and chirpy.

I need to exercise, but I genuinely don't feel amazing so maybe I just let this thing pass first. I only wish I knew if I had the bloody virus. I can't get my head around that I may never know. This is America. THIS is madness. You can spit into a tube and find out if your Great-Great-Great-Great Uncle Wally had a Spanish uncle, but you can't find out if you have flu? Well done, Trump. Nailing it.

At least the weather is improving. We did some bee-saving today because there are hundreds of docile ones on the lawn. I accidentally drowned one in the sugary water and felt like total shit about myself all day. Art put his hand on my shoulder and said, 'It's OK, Mummy, he didn't look like he was gonna make it.' And so I cried.

Why have I turned into a pathetic heap of blubbing nonsense?

I do think, as this goes on, things will fall into place. I have romantic ideas for isolated communes where we all get high while the kids play games like tiddlywinks and snap.

I have some good kaftans that would be perfect for such a scenario.

There are lots of people sending around ideas and activities to do with the kids. I need to get on it, rather than just resent the fact that to do any of those things involves me doing them too. But the reality is, if we fill three hours a day with solid activities, then the rest can be more fluid . . . free play, food, park, TV. So, I will do better. I just want to sit and read, or start my new novel, but these days aren't really working out that way. I guess what I'm most nervous of is that this school closure will become all about the kids. (Obviously, it *is* about the kids, but bear with me.) We must keep them motivated, fit, stimulated, but that leaves no time for us to work, does it? And if we can't work, then everything is a nightmare. So, hopefully schools are going to take that into account while they experiment with all this remote learning, and accept that the kids will get a bit less attention than they would at school.

WHAT IS HAPPENING.

In terms of activities, the school suggested that we cut out little leaves from paper and then the kids come up with things they are grateful for. (All Valentine, my two-year-old, ever says is 'whales'. All Art, age five, ever says is 'poo'.) You write what they say on them, then hook them onto twigs and put them in a vase. A little gratefulness tree. Quite cute. I think I can manage that. I'm grateful for weed gummies. Stick that on a leaf and smoke it.

My dog Potato is having the best week of his life because we are all home. Honestly, I wish I was a dog. No, I don't, I wish

I was a fish, because you can't get Covid-19 in the ocean. Can you? Oh God, what if it's in the water?

I did nail our Paddy's night dinner last night though. Corned beef and cabbage, with mashed potato and sweetcorn. It was yum. I think that tonight I'll make something extra special like . . . hmmm . . . hot dogs. Done.

Of course, this isn't all awful. I have two amazing boys who make me laugh all the time and happily occupy themselves when I ask them to. They are healthy, gorgeous and kind. It could be worse. There could be three of them.

OK, until tomorrow . . .

Love Dawn x

19 March
Isolation Update – The head in the cupboard

Today was considerably better and I attribute this to two factors:

1. I didn't bother getting my kids dressed, to avoid excess laundry.
2. I abandoned all efforts to educate them.

Turns out, if you totally give up on even attempting to nourish children intellectually, everyone is happier. What a revelation to come out of this strange and total shit-show of a time.

So . . . the day started well. I woke up at six something, but the kids didn't wake until seven thirty. They're going to bed late, and for this period that works fine by me; at that time in the morning, to sit and have a coffee before it all kicks off is nice. My favourite part of the day is by far the mornings. Everyone is generally quite happy to see each other after social distancing in our bedrooms throughout the night. Chris came up with the genius idea of putting a few chocolate cereal pieces into their regular healthy cereal, which means breakfast time is a dream. We don't give our kids much sugar because Art acts like me in the early 2000s in dingy Liverpool clubs at just the sniff of anything refined, so when they get any, they go into a trance.

I did playdough with the kids for nearly an hour. As expected, they squashed all the new playdough together until it turned brown and then threw it around the room yelling, 'I'm throwing poo-poo at you.' At first I shouted at them to stop, but soon realised, as I scraped it out of my hair, that I will never win. So instead I asked Alexa to play a 'Farty Party', and I pretended to do playdough poos all over the living room. This is where I am at.

NEXT, I ordered the kids a really cheap tent, which I popped up in their bedroom. They thought it was the greatest thing ever to happen for about forty-five minutes. While they were in it, I did a face mask, and then applied full make-up. There is so little I can control right now, but my eye make-up is something that no one can take away from me. I also wore double denim and didn't take my slippers off all day. If this is still going on when the weather cheers up, I'll bang out some kaftan action. I really feel that kaftans should be the traditional dress of isolation.

I gave Chris the morning off kids to get some work done, and right now Valentine is supposed to be napping. But he isn't. He is rubbing banana onto my bed sheets while I say, repeatedly, 'Mummy needs FIVE MINUTES.' He is not giving me those five minutes.

I'm defrosting some ready-made pesto chicken thing for dinner, and I had two packets of crisps with my lunch. It's 3 p.m. and Chris just walked in and gave me a margarita. What a guy!

Things I want to get better at during this time:

1. Calling family
2. Calling friends
3. Making podcasts
4. Bonding with my children (I realise that should probably have gone higher up the list)
5. Eating vegetables
6. Exercising
7. Not having meltdowns

But one day at a time.

Talking of days, what day even is it? I literally have no idea. Not that it matters.

OK, I'm going to go and turn the TV up for ten minutes, so that my kids can't hear me scream into a pillow. I hope your days went OK?

WHAT IS HAPPENING.

Love Dawn x

20 March
Isolation Update – My kid is green

OK, well today was marginally better. I put this down to me completely abandoning any sense of self and committing fully to the children's happiness and housework. Turns out, when not trying to do anything else, one can mother better.

This simply cannot go on.

I need to continue to work, when I can. But for today, I didn't even try, and we all got through it.

We started the day with some rock painting. You get paint, you collect rocks, and then you paint them. You let the paint dry, stick some googly eyes onto the rocks and then do not wash either child until bedtime, no matter what colour 90 per cent of their faces are. (Art – green, Valentine – red and black).

Donald Trump, our orange president, did a briefing this morning. LA is on almost a complete lockdown now. No shops, bars, bloody anything remain open. It's a ghost town. The weird thing is, I have become totally used to this and can't remember a time when I walked freely down a street, sneezing willy-nilly, instead of bathing in anti-bac every time the postman delivers a package. This is our new normal, for however long it lasts. Listening to Trump on the radio has never been pleasant, but now it's even worse, as every time he is telling us that more of America is closing down. People are losing their jobs by the second. It's the most devastating thing to hear. All we can hope is that we are wrong and, in a week or two, everything will be OK. Let's hold onto that thought for as long as we can. Because, as mad as the world is, and things keep getting worse, things could also be mad enough that they just get better and all of this madness will end.

I hope you're all OK.

Did I tell you that Chris panic-bought 200 worms? Well, give a two-year-old 200 worms and you have around twenty minutes of being able to think about something else. This activity was not relaxing. I rescued at least 40 worms from decapitation (got them all, no worms were harmed) and spent a very long time scraping soil off my carpet. Valentine named all the worms 'Mr Worm', and then was entirely over it by snack time. The worms are now in a large pot with moist soil, and I apparently have 200 more pets than I did yesterday. Great.

I ate crisps for lunch. With a side of cheese. I did not exercise.

I am making Jamie Oliver's chicken and mushroom pie for dinner. I am also digging out all of my trousers that have elastic waistbands because I wore jeans today and they hurt me.

I'm committed now to hunkering down. I've got lots of food. I can cook and deliver to anyone I know who gets stuck, and we could survive for a month. The reality of being in LA at the moment is that the last things open are the food shops. It's likely they will soon be closed too. Which is WILD.

Art (the five-year-old) misses his friends and has so much energy he can't burn off. I feel bad, but there isn't much we can do about it. I'm just trying to do as many activities as possible, and not lose my shit when he loses his.

Valentine, on the other hand, thinks it's awesome. We are potty-training him now – we thought we might as well – so the house is covered in his piss, as well as the cat's. By the time this is over it will probably be covered in mine too, to be honest.

OK, I'd better go. The kids are clawing at me again, and I want to cook the pie.

Sending love to you and yours, I really hope you're all OK,

Love Dawn x

Parenting – WHAT is that smell?

So I've been thinking about parenting a LOT over these past weeks, I mean, obviously, it's all I've been doing. It's just Chris and me doing 100 per cent of everything with the kids, the dog and the cat – and we are shocked at the constant stream of piss or shit coming out of at least one of them at any given time. I mean, what the HELL is happening? It's almost tempting to not feed anyone for an entire day, just to get a break from it.

I never thought I'd be married with two kids, because I was happily on track to be a single cat lady who wrote books in bed. There is rarely a day that goes by that I am not stunned by the life I appear to be living, but the good news is, I like it very much and find being a mother and a wife a largely riveting experience. Well, that is how I felt before the schools shut and I found myself a full-time stay-at-home mum without much warning.

It's important that I say at this point how much respect I have for full-time stay-at-home mums. One side effect of feminism that really breaks my heart, is how apologetic a lot of women feel they need to be for being just that. It is, quite simply, one of the hardest, most selfless jobs you can do. There is no 'clock-in at nine, leave at five'. It's an all-in, 24/7, every fucking day, SORRY, WHAT IS MY NAME AGAIN kind of job, and if there is any part of you that feels judgement towards a woman who is doing it, abandon those thoughts. Full-time mothers (parents, to be fair to the men who do it, of whom there are plenty) work harder than the rest of us. The point of feminism is to make sure that the women who don't want to do it have an equal amount of opportunity as the men who don't. It isn't there to make stay-at-home mothers feel less than – and if you ever witness that, call it out.

I must add that being a working parent is no joke either. There are rarely breaks. You get home from work after a long day and you begin the 'second shift' of giving the kids dinner and putting them to bed. And when you have small children, there is no such thing as a relaxing weekend.

Before lockdown I had pretty much been on a work deadline for the previous eighteen months. I'd get to my desk at 9 a.m. and not leave until 4.45 to collect the kids (on my days), working much later on the days it wasn't my turn. I'd be so caught up in it as my deadline approached that I'd barely look up to have a conversation. I'd go for turbo wees and eat lunch over my keyboard, to the point all the keys got stuck and I had to get another one. Two days a week Valentine would be downstairs in the day care that my workspace provided. I'd see him doing the music class on Wednesdays and feel awful that I wasn't down there with him like the other mums, but my workload wouldn't always allow it.

I'd dream of my writing being done, so I could take a few months off and just be at home with the kids. I craved it. Hoping that just one of my books would smash it out of the park, and that I'd make enough money to only have to write one a year and nothing else. Then I'd spend the rest of the time in a dreamy, homely bubble. Cooking amazing things and picking the kids up early. The reality was, I was in no position to take a few months off. If I stop working, I stop being paid, and it's taken years and years of writing at this level to get paycheques that actually contribute to our family. So, this was to be my pattern: bursts of intensity with bursts of less intensity. I have friends (men and women) who do jobs where it's high intensity all the time. We'd all talk about the dream of sabbaticals and breaks longer than a few weeks. We wanted month upon month of nothing but blissful family life.

Careful what you wish for. Hello, Mr Pandemic. (It's definitely a man.)

Why were there suddenly so many hours in a day? Why do kids aged two and five show such enthusiasm for things they are bored of five minutes later? Why does fifteen minutes feel like two hours? Why is it that everything fun makes loads of mess that is no fun to tidy up? When lockdown began, we didn't want Art to be sad and miss his friends, so we became his parents, teachers and best friends all in one. By the Friday of that first week, I had learned that the level of activity we were engaging in was completely unsustainable. I was not that woman, and as much as it pained me to admit it, I was not that mother.

It's a harsh experience to be confronted with the kind of mother you are. Mainly, perhaps, because you are labelling yourself. But we do that, women, don't we? We feel we have to fit into categories. The most prevalent categories that mothers are put into are 'good' or 'bad'. 'She's such a good mum.' Don't tell me you haven't said it about your friends.

So, let's work out which one I am, because on paper I kind of look OK. It's just a shame I don't exist only 'on paper'.

Reasons I am a great mother:

1. I am painstakingly dedicated to my kids' happiness.
2. I take their health very seriously and work hard on their food and nutrition.
3. I engage in hours of conversation, despite having relatively low interest, if any, in what they are talking about.
4. I have happily sacrificed my afternoon nap since having them.
5. I love them even more when they're ill and find great pleasure in nursing them back to health.
6. I have carved out a career that means I have a 98 per cent chance of being there for them if they need me.
7. I am utterly obsessed with them and think they are the two greatest humans who ever walked the earth.

Reasons I am a bad mother:

1. I am rubbish at playing.
2. When my kids do an impression of me, they shout, 'BE CAREFUL OF MY WINE.'
3. I fantasise about living in a cute two-bed flat in London with a couple of cats way more than I should.

Now, I realise that my 'bad mother' list is a lot shorter. But in the circumstances of lockdown, I realised that being a good player, in particular, is crucial. I know it's silly to buy into the perfect 'smug mum' scene on Instagram, but all I'd see were countless images of mums playing with their kids. Wild and adventurous games that they had invented, dens so extravagant a family of four could live in them, kids so happy they never wanted to see their friends again. And then there was me, out of ideas by Day 4, feeling like I didn't have the energy to keep two boys entertained, watching how my husband could play and play and play when all I ever seemed to say was 'in a minute', 'when I've done this . . .', 'after my wine is gone.' I do really try, but I get so tired, and that makes me feel so guilty that I internalise it and end up getting all disappointed in myself, so I have to go off and have a big think about life in a cupboard.

I spend a lot of time in cupboards.

I am unnecessarily defensive about childcare. This is because I live in Hollywood and am married to an actor. The media has painted a certain picture of parenting when you are in that situation. Multiple nannies, PAs and housekeepers. In many cases, this is entirely accurate. But not in ours. Before I start, I shall acknowledge the help that we have had.

When Art was five months old, we found Mary. Mary Moo, as I called her, was like an angel from above. A few years younger than me, a glorious mix of Ethiopian and Canadian, loving, fun, a great cook, a great teacher and an absolute breeze to have around. Mary worked full-time for us (average day: nine to five, Monday to Friday). It was like I had a sister-wife; we were both passionate about food and books and all sorts of other lovely things. She was brilliant in a crisis; if she was babysitting at night and one of the kids was sick in their beds, by the time Chris and I got home everything would be washed and the child would be wrapped up on the sofa with a bowl on their lap, somehow smiling, not even asking for us, because Mary was as good as it gets.

When Art was around eighteen months, he started going to a little day care close to our house, and Mary went to work for a friend of mine. A few years later, when I'd had Valentine, she came back to us and we did almost the same thing all over again. Although Valentine, being the second child, started at day care a little earlier. Because, ya know, second child vibes.

Last year Mary moved back to Canada to have a baby of her own. She'd been working for another family here for a year previous to that, and picking our kids up from school on Tuesdays and Thursdays then working through so Chris and I could go out for dinner. But she was still in our lives and the kids adored her so much, as did we. Finding someone to replace Mary has been hard, and I do wonder if it could ever feel the same. Luckily (when the bloody schools are open) we don't need a full-time person, so it's all about finding the perfect regular babysitters now (of which we've always had some lovely ones). I'm so grateful that we had that experience with her though; those baby years are hard work, especially when both parents are working and you don't have any family close by. To have someone you know your kids love in that way, makes everything a lot easier. And the way she loved them, urgh, it kills me that she left. There have also, of course, been other sitters and part-time help over the years, many of whom we love deeply. But Mary Moo, she was our Number One.

When I was pregnant with Art, I asked a friend here what advice she had for me, and her advice was 'hire a night nurse'. Don't get me wrong, I think night nurses sound amazing, but this made me cross. I wanted advice about how to hold my baby, feed my baby, get my baby to sleep. Not 'get staff'. It's not the advice I think people should give to expectant mothers. It doesn't fill anyone with confidence, it doesn't make them think they can do it. I tell any friends who are having babies, if they ask, to see how it goes, and then get all the help they feel they need when they need it. I give the same advice for the birth. See how it goes and get the epidural if you need it. I find all of this planning for worst-case scenarios really depressing. There is so much fear instilled into people about having kids. *Birth will tear you apart and you'll never sleep again*. It's true, both of those things might happen, and it could be really terrible and often is. But also, it might not be. Birth might be the best thing you ever did, you might even be able to jump on a trampoline afterwards (I can't, but you might). And your baby might be a sleepy one, and you'll wonder what all the fuss was about. Hope for the best and do what you need to do when and if you need it. That's my advice, not that anyone asked.

Personally, when I have too much childcare, I start to feel like the nanny when it's my turn to take care of them. It's happened a few times when I've been on a really intense deadline and Mary and Chris have been doing the lion's share. By the time Saturday morning comes, I'm all out of kilter with them and it's really stressful. I think a lot of parents who work long hours would probably say the same thing. The less time you spend with your kids, the harder it can be to spend time with them. However, we both have to work, and that is exactly the shitty 'guilt' feeling that people talk about. I swore I'd never feel it when I got pregnant, but I do, I feel it all the time. When we got childcare, I felt guilty that they were in the house with her, while I sat in the office doing my job. IT IS SO STUPID. And it goes on . . . If for any reason it hasn't been me who baths them and puts them to bed for say, three nights in a row, I feel awful. If I am not the one organising their meals, I feel guilty. If I have a busy work week and then there is something happening at the weekend which means I needed more help, I feel mean. I know Chris goes through exactly the same thing. His job can often take him away from home for long periods of time, him hopping back at the weekends. He parents harder than ever while he is home to make up for being away, but of course he feels guilty that he is away at all. But hard work affords us a life we all love. I know the kids won't remember the times he is away, or the nights I have to work late, and they'll just have the happiest memories of when we are at home. But still, guilty guilty guilty, all the bloody time.

People say parenting is hard and there are so many reasons why that is. The literal, physical effort that it takes to look after small children. The emotional effort of taking care of older ones. The lack of sleep. The financial pressure. The need to reach a compromise with your parenting partner, if there is one. The working, the socialising that you deserve but don't get to do. Balancing it all can feel impossible at times. Guilt is just a part of it. Whether it's about the kids, your relationship, or your friends that you never see and can't be there for. Guilt. All the time. I've got so used to it being a part of my day. At some point, before I go to sleep, I will inevitably feel like total shit about something.

That was until lockdown happened. I don't think I'll feel guilty about going to work ever again. Also, I want childcare every weekend until they're eighteen. And I want a night nurse – not for the kids, but for me. Because you know what, fuck it.

Things I know now that I didn't know before lockdown:

1. Toddlers are not to be left alone with worms.
2. Hiding in cupboards is key.
3. Lego is HARD.

PIECE TWO

My People

24 March
Isolation Update – 'There has been a terrible problem'

I am stunned to be sharing this information with you all, but I think I enjoyed today. What is most peculiar is that I didn't start drinking until 4 p.m. That means there were nine hours of daytime that I genuinely didn't hate. This could be because of three things:

1. I was still drunk from yesterday.
2. I have totally given up on myself.
3. My friends are the best.

The kids slept until 7 a.m., which felt like a holiday. Chris and I take it in turns to get up and do breakfast. This morning he said, 'Whose turn is it?' I said, 'Yours,' and he went into the kitchen muttering about waffles. It took me a moment to remember that he had made the kids waffles for breakfast yesterday, and it was actually my morning. I sent him back to bed with a coffee, and popped some bread in the toaster. I'd slept well, so was more than happy to get up. Aren't I being lovely and affable so far?

In that short moment where I lay in bed, thinking I had the morning off, the dull ache of relentlessness consumed me. Here we go again, another day of exactly the same thing. More drawing, more playdough, more throwing their squidgy fake-poo toy at the wall and howling with laughter as it falls to the ground. More time on my hands and knees scraping food off the floor. More time in front of a mirror scraping food out of my hair. As I took those thoughts in, I could have cried. But I didn't cry. I reminded myself that this might be my only chance to spend this much time with my kids, without work pulling me away. To enjoy it. To take it on. Embrace it. And so, I did. I went into the kitchen with a smile on my face, and I managed to maintain it for most of the day.

As always, while I saw to the kids, I was also on WhatsApp. Because of the time difference with the UK, I usually wake up to a flurry of messages. This morning, a friend in London asked me how I was feeling about Caroline, she was checking in. I told her the truth: it still hurts like hell, but I am powering on because I have no choice. I mean, I do have a choice – I could totally fall apart. But I have a family to hold together, so I can't do that. Sometimes it feels like my WhatsApp groups are the places where I can sink my true feelings. If I feel tears coming, I message a friend, maybe even a few at once, and say, 'I'm having a bad moment. I can't do this. I miss her too much.' And almost immediately I am met with support. Words that pull me together. Or sometimes their own sadness is reflected back, which reminds me I am not alone in mine. I think one reason I have never really committed to therapy is because I don't see what more I could get out of it than what I get from my girlfriends. Whenever there's a heavy hand pressing down on one of my shoulders, I feel it lift a little the moment one of my friends gets in touch to ask me if I am OK.

Anyway, on to the rest of the day (what day even is it?). I did twenty minutes on the Peloton. I think that is my limit on the amount of time I can work out before I get really cross and hate everyone. It's as if that twenty minutes releases just the right amount of pheromones, or whatever the fuck exercise releases, and it suits me just fine. If I try to do more than that, I just won't keep it up. I promised myself that I would do twenty minutes every morning while this isolation continues.

We all know that this will never happen.

Admittedly, I totally forgot to educate my kids today. Again. We are supposed to log in and watch all the videos the school has made. Although I appreciate the effort, I do think these first few weeks have to be about adjustment. For most of you in the UK, today was your first day of 'Remote Learning'. It's full-on, isn't it? Especially if you have multiple kids. That's where I was at last week, and on Tuesday I had a massive meltdown and felt really scared of it all. It seemed so much, so soon. School's cancelled and BAM, we're supposed to follow a syllabus. I am lucky that Art is only five and the stuff they are asking us to do is minimal. They don't even learn to read here at five. Which is why I am being quite chilled about it. I am not deliberately trying to hold my kid back. Promise.

The WhatsApp group for Art's class is alive with swearing. Messages like 'NO NO NO' in capitals. 'FUCK THIS' or 'THIS IS IMPOSSIBLE'. 'My kid hates this' and 'I need my computer back' are on a loop. We constantly question how long this will last. Most of us need to work but we're having to guide our kids through tasks set by the school. No one can quite believe what we are being asked to do. Remote learning with a five-year-old? That's as bad as it gets.

The mum group is comforting though, and they're a fun bunch. It's nice to know Art isn't the only one in his class with a parent who is tearing their hair out.

I downloaded Demi Moore's autobiography, which I listened to in the kitchen while making one of the 638,909 meals I had to make today. It's good, I recommend it. She's had a mad old life, and she gets all juicy about her marriages, which is fun.

I hate baking, but I know kids love it. I defrosted some pastry this morning, and the kids rolled it out and we cut it into shapes. Valentine ate raw egg then spat it all over the pastry, then Art and I sprinkled cheese on top. I put them in the oven and they were yummy. Little cheesy parcels. We had them with crisps, so probably have scurvy now, but according to the radio we are all GOING TO DIE anyway, so what does it matter?

Valentine took all his clothes off and pissed in the tent. A horse-like piss, that created a shallow pool that took up the entire tent. He thinks potty training is about finding the most inventive place to take a slash. Anywhere but the goddam toilet, apparently. I put on a really bossy voice and said, 'Do you want me to put a nappy on you, like a baby?'

He just said yes.

After that he disappeared outside and came back a while later holding a cup. 'Mummy, there has been a terrible problem.' (He is two.) He handed me the cup.

There were three dead bees in it.

'Valentine, did you hurt the bees?' I asked.

'Or they would sting me,' was all he said. I pushed him to add a few words to the beginning of that sentence, but no, 'Or they would sting me' was all I got.

I may never know what happened to those poor bees. Oh dear.

It was 8.30 by the time I eventually got them both into bed. It was what I think you call in parenting 'a total shitshow'. But they are down. Anyway, Chris is doing a Zoom poker night, and I just did a 'House Party' with some mums from Art's school class. I can be terrible at things like this. Zoom chats freak me out a bit, especially with people I don't know very well. I'd said I couldn't do it at first, then last minute I jumped on and I'm so glad I did. It's good to connect with people who understand what you're going through. I still can't believe I am a mum of two with other mum friends. Life is so surreal. Luckily, I found cool ones.

Night-night or morning, depending on where you are!

Love Dawn x

26 March
Isolation Update – Don't fuck with eggs

Quick question before we crack on: how many more memes do I have to pretend to find funny before this crisis ends? Also, a friend of mine just told me she is dating a 'memer'.

THAT is a person who makes memes for a living. People get paid to meme? WHAT IS HAPPENING?

I actually love chatting to my single friends about their bonkers dating lives. Dating a memer in isolation? Of course, I made lots of jokes about them communicating via the medium of meme and asked if he continually quoted his own memes during lovemaking. She found it funny, because she is my friend. And she knows if she says ridiculous things like 'I am dating a memer' to someone like me, there will be consequences.

I woke up at 7.30, just before everyone else. I came into the kitchen and boiled the kettle, excited for a moment's peace. Then I wandered into the living room to find a pile of cat sick next to the sofa. Behind it, some shit. Seconds later, Valentine flew in lathered in snot. Right after that, Art called me because he'd wet the bed. Before the kettle was even boiled, I had dealt with multiple urine, shit, snot or vomit incidents. This is not what I signed up for when I married a movie star. I wonder how different it would have been if I'd married a memer instead.

Over breakfast (cereal and mango) the kids had a fight with their spoons. It started off fun, but soon turned violent. I told them they mustn't fight, then they threw their spoons across the room and, for a moment there, I considered getting Lilu's sick out of the bin, rubbing their spoons in it, then giving them back to them. (Lilu is the mad Siamese cat who has lived with me for sixteen years – more on her later.) I managed to restrain myself. But I did tell them that if they did it again, I would give them both chickenpox. That shut them up. (They are immunised, I'm not THAT cruel. Also I said it in a jokey voice.) OK, OK, I feel bad.

When I had fed them, and released them from the table, I fried a couple more eggs, one for Chris and one for me. Valentine came over and demanded to eat some of mine. I gave it to him, because I felt guilty about the chickenpox. He ate it, then spat it out into my hand.

Who the actual hell are these people?

I FaceTimed my dad, which was lovely. I usually go weeks without speaking to him. It's a terrible habit I have fallen into, and one that I always want to correct. This week, we have spoken every day. I really do believe that this will bring the love out in a lot of people. I realise the opposite is also true, but it's making me want to connect more with the people I love. I am trying hard to do that.

I wore bunchies in my hair today, adding an element of cuteness to my ageing look. I have enjoyed it immensely and will be experimenting with new hairstyles as the days plod on. I was due a haircut before all this happened and am weeks away from no longer having a bob. Isn't that just so exciting for us all? I'll keep you posted every step of the way.

I did a strong eye, despite the order not to leave the house. I also wore a top with sparkles on it. No one can tell me I don't bring the party to isolation.

By 2.22 in the afternoon I was longing for a drink but was determined to get to at least 3 p.m. But then my sister FaceTimed me from the UK; she was really drunk and talking absolute nonsense about God knows what. She was quite shouty, and when I put her on the phone to Art she sounded like a mad aunty in a comedy movie, so I told Art to go play while I listened to her rabbit on about some planting she'd done that day. What was nice about her call was that it made my need to drink feel more appropriate. Sometimes the eight-hour time difference can be very useful.

School recommended a game where you put an egg in a zip-lock bag, fill the bag with whatever you can find, then drop the bag and see if you've managed to protect the egg from smashing. I was like: EGGS ARE LIKE SACRED CRYSTALS RIGHT NOW, WHY THE HELL WOULD I RISK SMASHING ONE?

We didn't do the experiment. Which makes this Day 12 of not educating my child. He's FINE.

There was plenty more pant-pissing throughout the day, so I ended up taking off Valentine's trousers altogether. He thought this was brilliant and spent most of the afternoon on all fours with his ass in the air. I always tell my kids to put their bums away, not encouraging it. Otherwise all we would talk about would be bums and poo. But occasionally, when they least expect it, I pull a mooner just so they think I'm the coolest mum ever. Works a treat. Gets me loads of hugs.

My friend Rebecca made me a loaf of sourdough and dropped it round. The bread was UNREAL. Like, proper fluffy English bread, rather than the weird, sweet, rubbery stuff you get here. She stood outside with a mask on and we chatted, and it was amazing. But I wanted more. I miss my friends. I want to hug them. It really devastates me to stand a few feet away from someone I love, not being able to touch them, and having to wear a mask. It's so weird. Our house has always been full of friends. Most Sundays since we have lived in this house we've had people over. It's the party house. Now it's the farty house.

I miss drinking with grown-ups. Kids are way more judgey.

OK, that's it from me for tonight,

Love Dawn x

Friends Are for Life, Not Just for Lockdown

In 'normal' times, I can take friendship a little for granted. I'm rubbish at calling people back, I don't arrange nearly enough dinners. I like to entertain at home so invite everyone round, but I miss out on seeing the people who can't make it. When isolation is over, I want to do better. Weekly dinners with my girls, more one-on-ones and lunches and brunches. Because this time of chaos has shown me just how vital my female friendships truly are. Multiple WhatsApp groups have become daily therapy sessions where we can offload about parenting, marriage and work woes; all delivered with unrelenting honesty and received with judgement-free eyes and thumbs.

These are the major WhatsApp groups in my life:

Group One

LA DICKHEADS – this is made up of my sister Jane and best mate Lou. It makes me happier than anything else that I have them both in the same virtual place and that they get on so well. Jane and Louise being friends is magic. We each have two boys. Lou is in Australia, Jane Bristol, me LA. The chat is funny, often self-inflammatory, rarely self-deprecating, and endlessly varied. We tell each other the things we do well, like meals we cook, or things we do around the house. There is no need for us to apologise for acknowledging our greatness, we want to hear it all.

Jane is a garden designer in Bristol (message me if you need one) and Louise runs a cinema in Melbourne (if you're there, you must all go, it's called the Thornbury Picture House – shameless best mate plug). Their common ground seems to be taking the piss out of me. This can range from the position I sleep in (face down with my arms by my side; LITERALLY the unsexiest position possible), or my obsession with my appearance (often centred around my eyebrows or hair straighteners), or my appetite (often centred around the sheer magnitude of it). I love it all. No one on this earth knows me better than Jane and Louise. I can be 100 per cent myself at all times. They are the only people I fart in front of. Unless it's an accident.

Group Two

US LOT – on here we have Kelly, Michelle and Mel. These are my LA besties. We all have young kids, and we text all day every day about kids, family life and vaginas. The chat here is random and more about the day-to-day grind. It's funny and supportive and a great place to bitch about the small stuff. Michelle works in business. Mel works for a start-up called Daily Karma, and she is also a doula (she watched Valentine come out of me) and a badass women's rights activist. And Kelly is an ex popstar turned singer/songwriter with a voice like an angel who is currently learning how to perform sound baths. We all have two kids each. Workwise, I rarely have any idea what Mel and Michelle are talking about, and Kelly is all earthy and spiritual. They are *all* quite earthy and spiritual actually. Kelly lives a bit further away, but Mel and Michelle and I live streets away from each other, so it was really weird not seeing them as much in person in the early days of isolation. Even though we were socially distant, we still felt close. We'd hear the same helicopters circling the neighbourhood and bump into each other sometimes. These guys are very important to Chris and me. None of us live near our families, so we are all aunts and uncles to each other's kids. Our kids have grown up together. And as soon as the restrictions began to lift a little, they were the first people we wanted the kids to see.

Group Three

DRUNKEN TURTLES – this one is a real breakthrough group from 2020. Art's school year was called the 'Sea turtles'. We had a 'mum dinner' that I was terrified about, but we all got on great and then set up a WhatsApp group, which is a real hoot. I'd been terrified about the dinner because I had thoughts like, 'just because we have kids doesn't mean we have anything in common'. Blah blah blah. I was still in total denial that I was a forty-year-old mother of two. I'd had years of negative 'school gate' chat drilled into me from other mums, TV shows, articles, etc., and I didn't want to be a part of it. I wanted to be the kind of mum who dropped my kid off and picked him up, no more involvement. I didn't want my life to become about PTAs and school fundraisers. BOOOORRRIIINNNGGGGG. I presumed ALL other mothers were the exact opposite of me and that all we would talk about at the dinner would be the kids and the teachers.

Turns out, I am the only asshole in the group, because all the mums are totally awesome, way cooler than I could ever be, and all interesting, hilarious and super smart. And I realised as I chomped down on the best chicken parmesan I have ever had in my life, that I was ready to be a forty-year-old mother of two, and that talking about the kids with like-minded people was actually fun. I love these women. I am delighted to be one of them. That night we all ate too much, drank too much and massively over-shared. My favourite kind of evening.

The WhatsApp chat is fun.

The chat ranges from parenting to gyno appointments, rants about Trump, recommendations for local stuff, TV shows and medical matters. We also have one paediatric doctor in the group, so she is amazing at answering any Covid-related questions we have. There's a manager of some major pop stars and a sex therapist too, among many other interesting people. And that is what I have come to love about being a mum with a kid at school; you get thrust in with people you might never otherwise meet and, if you embrace it, it can be really, really fun. I have a lot to thank this group for. They kicked off my experience of being a 'school mum' with a blast. I'm finally really into it – it's just a shame the bloody school has been shut down.

Group Four

BEST CREW EVER – this one consists of my friends Gemma, Ophelia and Josie. We were all close to Caroline and every now and then one of us pops up in this group to say, 'Hey, I feel sad, how you guys doing?' and it's lovely. When you lose a friend, friendship becomes everything.

After the funeral, we knew we had to be there for each other. It's obviously been hard, especially with me being in America, and the world being in lockdown. But we all loved her so much and this group is there when any of us need it. All my friends have been there for me this year, but the ones who knew Caroline like I did have been very important. This chat group is like a cushion of warm, cosy support; a massive comfort in very testing times.

I also want to give a shout out to Nancy, Carrie, Cam, Shawnta, Kristen, Jo, Dee and many more . . . You know who you are. I have so many brilliant women that I call my friends. I know that makes me very lucky and I feel it deep in my bones. There is a good chance that none of them will read this book, but if you do, I LOVE YOU and thanks.

I believe female friendship makes the world a better place. Men operate more individually, striving for personal success. That is a huge generalisation, but I'm pretty certain it is true. A man's mentality is to hunter-gather and provide for himself and his family. A woman's mentality is to connect with others and build community. We spread ourselves further, we lean on each other more. When you share yourself with other women, and you allow them to do the same, you find your power. The women in my life are my backbone. I tell my friends everything, always, all of them. The second a thing happens, my thumbs get into action and tell them. The immediate inpouring of support is something I have come to rely on.

Here are the reasons why female friendship is so important:

- You can have honest feedback that doesn't cause a fight. Honesty in romantic relationships can be hard because you have to live right on top of the emotional consequences. Personally, I tend to hold things back and let them fester, which is a disaster. I am much better at speaking up in my friendships than I am in marriage, which, as you can imagine, is really fun for my husband.
- I'd argue that my best friends know me better than anyone. No matter how close I am to Chris, there are things about me he will never understand because he isn't female. The way I talk to him is different, the way I open up to him is different. The way I rely on him is different. I love the way he protects me and makes me feel so secure. But the relationship is different, even he wouldn't deny that. I see it often in the depths of chats we have about certain things. For example (and this is a frivolous example, because I am not here to share my actual problems), I was telling him about a dream that I had and saw him, quite rightfully, glaze over. So I got on the chat with Mel, Michelle and Kelly and told them instead. I was immediately given a deep analysis of the dream and ideas and suggestions as to where it came from and what inspired it. THAT is what girlfriends do. It isn't the husbands' fault, it's just that we are wired differently. I'm cool with it, because I have my girls. My female friends are my emotional support animals. Even when they only exist on text, I need them just the same.
- A great friendship is like having all the best boyfriends

> you ever had merged into one person, without the pressure of having to live with them or maintain a sex life when you're tired. It's why losing one is so awful. It's not just one person, it's a collection of memories, conversations and laughter that connect you to someone. A friendship is a link in a chain, but with this particular design, you can't replace it if it breaks. I realised immediately that the gap Caroline left could not be filled. Our isolation texts would have been hilarious. I imagine them in my head all the time. Instead, I knew I had to make the absolute most of everyone else. Work harder at those relationships and do my best to keep them going.

In lockdown, it all happened on my phone. The WhatsApp groups were like unscrewing a bottle of something fizzy. Each message relieved a little bit of pressure, provided a moment of relief, a reassurance that the female energy in my life will always be there, even when one is gone. In such sadness there was solidarity. I felt very lucky to be a woman.

I feel sad for my two sons that they will never feel the power of female friendship for themselves. The least I can do is surround them with mine. As soon as this is over, regular 'Ladies Nights' will be a feature in our house. I want Art and Valentine to feel the energy of that solidarity. The laughter, the support, the warmth and maybe, most importantly, the incredible display of sensational vintage kaftans.

PIECE THREE

Food. All of the Food

31 March
Isolation Update – Sausages and dresses

Well, here we are again. Another update where I try to fill a page by making absolutely nothing sound interesting. We made it through the weekend. It was nice and felt different because neither of us tried to work. It was DIY, sorting shit out and childcare central around here for two whole days. You can imagine how much I drank.

Yesterday, I cooked our favourite dinner – corned beef and cabbage with a leek and potato gratin. It was LOADED with cheese and oozing with fat and we ate it all and loved every mouthful. Sundays HAVE to be about food, right?

I'd done a Lizzo Peloton class in the morning. It was thirty minutes of hard cycling JUST to Lizzo music. I tried to sing along but could hardly breathe, so afterwards I put on her album and had a kitchen disco while I grated cheese. I felt smug as hell and kept singing 'Feeling smug as hell' to the tune of 'Feeling Good as Hell'. Perfect. It's exactly what Lizzo would want.

I chatted to my dad on Sunday, and he told me a marvellous story about how he was on FaceTime with my sister and felt what he thought was a big mole on his face. He got very upset about it, and while on the phone to Jane looked in the mirror. 'Oh no, I've got a . . . no, wait . . .' He then realised it wasn't a mole but a Coco Pop. Him and Jane then totally lost it and I was SO happy to hear that such laughter existed in this weird and unsociable time. He couldn't wait to tell me about it. And I laughed for about an hour. Until Valentine wet his pants again. Urgh.

We ran out of eggs yesterday and I honestly felt like I was in the war and soldiers were going to come around with tickets that would get me dairy products.

That isn't what happened. I just went to the shop and got some more eggs.

It did make me think what the perfect emergency supplies would be. Some obvious, some that you only realise you need when the chance of purchasing them is dramatically reduced.

When the pandemic hit, the shelves were so empty. Before I left for Caroline's funeral, I had a small but genuine fear of not getting home. So I stocked up for Chris and the boys, because I needed to know that they would be alright if they weren't able to buy food. I think this is what they call being a 'Mumma Bear'. I went to Target, aiming to buy tins and dried food and loo roll, stuff like that, but the shelves were empty. It was frightening. Nothing had been announced at that point, the word 'lockdown' wasn't yet a common term on everyone's lips.

I managed to get some tinned vegetables, some weird-shaped pasta that no one else wanted, kitchen roll – the useless and totally unabsorbent kind – flour, long-life milk, jars of peaches and other random shit that I thought Chris could fathom some meals out of, if they got stuck. I told him he had enough to survive on for a week, if this 'lockdown' thing, whatever that was, actually did happen. (AND OF COURSE IT DID, IT HAPPENED WITH BLOODY BELLS ON.)

So I've been thinking, here is my ultimate list and what I will be putting in airtight containers in our basement when we move house. I reckon, with all of this, we could survive about ten days, no problem.

Loo roll, kitchen roll, cleaning supplies. Toothpaste, soap, shampoo and razors. Lots of sunscreen. Baby wipes, laundry detergent and dish soap.

Cooking oil AND olive oil, flour, baking soda, baking powder, yeast, sugar, coffee, teabags, long-life nut milk (always makes me laugh), dried fruit, egg substitute. Salt and pepper. Ketchup, mayonnaise, mustard, chocolate. A huge bag of rice and a whopping great bag of pasta. A few different shapes, because the shape DOES matter, depending on the sauce. (I still have standards in lockdown.) Japanese panko breadcrumbs (if the kids are refusing to eat the basic food, they might eat it if you cover it in breadcrumbs and fry it). Apple juice. Rice cakes. Honey, Marmite, huge jar of peanut butter, big box of Cheerios.

Tins of peaches, pineapple, coconut milk, tomatoes, tomato paste, ready-chopped garlic (hate it normally, but I cannot survive more than twenty-four hours without garlic), baked beans, chickpeas, peas and a few random kinds of beans for flavourless vegan stews if shit gets really bad.

For the freezer: pretentious beef hot-dog sausages (no butts and eyeballs). Bread. Tortilla wraps. Individually wrapped steaks. Chicken thighs. Bratwurst. Beef mince. Tilapia fillets. As many bags of frozen fruit and vegetables as you can get in. Butter, ready-made pastry and a few frozen pizzas. Packets of ham, turkey and sliced cheese. Frozen chopped onion.

For the kids – lollipops, so I can shut them up in a crisis. Fruit jerky. Loads of healthy-ish granola bars. Seaweed. Cartons of apple juice.

PLUS, so many crisps that you can barely get into the basement. Like, all of the crisps. Build this collection over time. Every time you go to a shop, buy some, and add to the stock. DO NOT be complacent about the crisp supply, just keep plugging away at it. For your entire life.

AND THEN . . .

10 x Casamigos tequila (it's the brand George Clooney created. He is my boyfriend.)
5 x fresh lime juice
3 x triple sec
12 x good quality Spanish red wine
12 x dry, crisp white wine
Plastic cups in case things get smashed in an earthquake
A shitload of weed gummies

OK, that's it.

Reading that, it might actually be quite a fun week.

Right, I'm off for a margarita and I'll make something FABULOUS in the kitchen. Or maybe I'll just smash a bag of Kettle chips and whack some fish fingers in the oven.

IS IT TOMORROW YET?

Love Dawn x

1 April
Isolation update – SUCH a Good Mum

I got all 'Instagram Mum' on Saturday and we painted terracotta pots with leftover paint samples. They look amazing and the kids loved doing it. I will be proud of myself for the rest of my life for doing an hour of 'crafts' with my children. The pots are so cute and really brighten up the garden.

I'm taking the wins where I can get them.

I've never been someone to get annoyed by the 'Smug Mum' scene on Instagram that gets everyone so riled up. When women post those perfect family photos, where the mummy and daddy are laughing at the kid playing in a pile of mud but it's in portrait mode and the mum is close by with a towel at the ready and a load of LOLS and the caption reads something ridiculous like 'I love it when he gets all messy. He's a kid, it's what they do. Let them play with mud!' I don't get annoyed because we all know what happens next.

She goes in to retrieve the child from the mud. The child goes ballistic and smothers the mum's pretty white dress in mud that she later discovers has tar in it and will never wash out. The child's muddy hands go into the mother's mouth, so the mother eats the mud. The father tries to help, to which the mother screams 'YOU DON'T NEED TO FIX THIS' because she harbours so much resentment towards him because he only took two weeks' paternity and spent the whole time playing online poker. Eventually, the mother gets the child out of the mud, her dress and face soiled. The child then scratches its long, untrimmed nails down her face, leaving what will probably be a permanent scar. She drags the child kicking and screaming to the bath, where she showers it down while it thrashes around so badly that it smacks its head on the side of the bath, getting a golf-ball level bump that she has to disclaim on a form when she drops the child at day care the next day. She tries to dress the child as it kicks her in the tits and face until the mother is so despondent she puts the TV on and collapses on the sofa, only to be jumped on by the other kids that she had forgotten to feed. A few hours later, when she is exhausted, weepy and possibly quite hammered, she looks at her phone and sees the lovely photo her husband took before all of the above happened and she decided to divorce him. So she posts it on Instagram, and allows the lie of perfection to cloud her reality. The husband says 'Shall we go to bed' and she says yes and follows him. They don't have sex, the baby wakes in the night and the mother is sick because there was norovirus in the mud she ate.

HAVE I PAINTED A GOOD PICTURE THERE??

We all know that is what parenting young kids looks like.

But still, I'm proud of the pots.

In darker news, I got really pissed off to hear how many people in America (California especially) have rushed out to buy guns. People who would usually be 'anti-guns'. Everyone is terrified that they will be attacked by people who have lost everything. I HATE IT. I have a zero-gun tolerance rule, no matter who the fuck you are. Same rules for all. Also, nothing bad has happened yet. NO TO GUNS. The fear, the paranoia, it has to stop. I hate it. You've been asked to stay home so you don't catch flu, you don't need a fucking gun. What are you going to do, shoot the virus?

Makes me SO MAD.

(Imagine if, after writing that, I get murdered in my own home by a maniac that I could have shot with a gun.)

What will be will be. I will not have a gun in my house, ESPECIALLY because of my kids. Even though we had a shotgun when I was a kid, and I was amazing at hitting Coke cans at the bottom of the garden. Reason ONE I don't want a gun in the house . . . KIDS LIKE PLAYING WITH THEM.

I hated everyone when I found out they were buying guns. EVERYONE.

We do have baseball bats around though – we're not fucking stupid.

Remember when I painted those pots?

Love Dawn x

2 April
Isolation update – Licking the cheese

My cheese intake has more than quadrupled since isolation started. I have it in sandwiches, on forks, I lick it off knives, and sometimes I just stand next to the fridge and eat it directly from the door.

Marmite and cream cheese sandwiches though, mmmmmm.

I risked my life in the supermarket today and got loads of nice food. It's literally all we have that changes each day, so I'm going for it with yummy meals. Also, I've introduced a 4 p.m. charcuterie board. My kids are gonna be such wankers.

Seriously though, my 'thing' in life is food. More so than dresses, it's so important to me. I think I have a really emotional connection to it because I lived with my grandparents until I was ten, and all they ever cooked was ham, egg and chips type stuff (don't get me wrong, I LOVE that food). So when I moved in with my aunty and uncle, and they were serving up fish with capers, whole crabs, oysters, steaks, full Sunday roasts, GODDAM avocado mousse starters, my taste buds got the kind of wake-up call that changes you forever. Food became my obsession, as cooking is now. My favourite part of every day is making the food we eat. I shop, I cook, I follow recipes and I make shit up. It makes me SO happy..

I don't know if any of you ever listened to my podcast series 'Get It On'. It was an interview show where I asked my guests why they wear what they wear. At the end of every episode, I asked them: If there was one photo that represented who you are the most, what would it be? For me, it was simple. The photo would be me, in my favourite vintage Ossie Clarke dress, getting a tray of sausages out of the oven. I picked this image (the photo doesn't have to exist, you can make it up) because it's about my love of vintage dresses, but also the big tray of sausages suggests I am cooking for a bunch of people. Which is me at my absolute happiest.

So, I ask you, what would you be doing in your photo?

Love Dawn x

3 April
Isolation Update – Stupid orange things: no!

It was Chris's morning with the kids, so I lay in bed like a lush, drinking coffee until 8 a.m., then did the Lizzo Peloton class and ate bacon to make up for it. I think that is what they mean by a 'balanced diet'?

Nailing it.

I took the kids to the park today. Our usual spot (the baseball pitch) was empty, which was great. Valentine had a meltdown within thirty seconds, and Art followed with an absolute belter a few minutes later. Both sat on the edge of the baseball pitch, next to a little plastic orange triangle, screaming with high emotion about God knows what. Little did I know, but two big men who wanted bigger muscles had put a row of those orange things in a line to create some sort of circuit for their exercises. They got really cross at me for bringing kids into their situation. They were grunting and sweating out of their foreheads at me. All 'Urgh' and 'You're in our spot.' Please see my problem . . . I now have FOUR men being grumpy with me in the park. I asked mine to get up, but they wouldn't. So the two workout freaks huffed and puffed some more. I tried to lift one of mine, saying loudly, so the men heard, hoping they'd cut me some slack, 'Come on, we are in the way.' But the men got madder at me and looked at me like I was totally ruining their life. I got upset. My kids get out the house for less than an hour a day and these men are pissed off that they are within a foot of their stupid orange cone? FUCK. OFF.

I suddenly felt rage. Real rage. The two men tried to stare me down. The park was practically empty, they could see my kids were being assholes and that I had a lot on my plate, but they didn't care. MEN! They could have just moved their STUPID orange plastic thing five feet to the right, and all would have been well. But they didn't. (I would have done it myself, but it could have had coronavirus on it.) They looked at me like vermin, because I dared to have children. So, I Mumma-beared the shit out of it.

'OWN THE FUCKING PARK, DO YOU?' I screeched to the men.

On that note, both of my children stood up and walked away. I was left, quivering, livid, determined. The two men pretended not to notice me, but I stood firm. 'There is all that space over there,' I continued. I then flicked my hand violently in the direction of grass. They came over, picked up the orange thing and moved it. Easy. I followed my children over to the nearby tree they were now hiding behind.

'Are you cross, Mummy?' Art said.

'Not with you, baby,' I told him. 'But those men are ASSHOLES.'

Something tells me I won't be Iceland's #mumoftheyear this time round.

We found another corner of the park, and an old lady stood around twenty feet from us doing lunges. She had a lot of questions: 'Are you a full-time stay-at-home mum?' she asked. To which I said, 'Yes.' Because right now I am, and I couldn't be bothered to explain otherwise. 'What does your husband do?' she asked. 'He's an actor,' I replied. She then made all sorts of assumptions.

'I'm an acting teacher,' she said.

'Oh nice,' I replied.

'Tell him to call me, I'll teach him how to act.'

'You know, he's doing OK, actually. But thanks so much.'

'He needs lessons,' she said.

'He's doing fine, really,' I said.

But she wouldn't let it go. So I ended up yelling – because she was quite far away – 'It's FINE, he is CHRIS O'DOWD.' Joggers stopped jogging. Dogs stopped barking. Trees stopped swaying. She yelled back 'WHO?' And then jogged off.

SO awkward.

I had tequila at 4 p.m. and I think it saved my life. I also smoked some pot then smashed half a saucisson and a massive lump of brie. BEFORE dinner. That's where I'm at.

LA announced that school is out until September. It is full-on news. Awful, in a way. Wonderful, in another. I am trying to be good at this. Trying to imagine the story I tell of the PANDEMIC in ten years.

'It was a weird and scary time, but we got through it. It was months of family time that we've never had since. It was special. We barbecued, sat naked in the paddling pool, watched movies, ate chips. We painted each other's nails, played with the dog, put the kids to bed then watched loads of great movies. We played backgammon and had lots of sex, made up games, taught the kids how to read. I tried new recipes, we ate some amazing food, I took care of the old lady next door, FaceTimed my family loads, did as much as we could for people who were struggling and tried to write some really funny things. It was a weird time, but we did it, and we had a lot of fun.'

My reality is NOT THAT, but I am going to try to aim for it, even a little.

What would you like your PANDEMIC story to be, and how likely is it that you think it will happen?

Love Dawn x

3 April
Isolation Update – Let me squeeze your finger

I don't mean to go on about this, but do you remember that time I painted those terracotta pots with my kids?

An absolute triumph.

Such a good mum.

I literally ran out of ideas thirty seconds after that, and can't be bothered to do anything right now, but nothing takes away from the fact that I did it.

Is it 2023 yet? Because maybe this will be over by then.

Isn't it funny that all those people who get Botox won't be able to get it while this is happening? I wonder if Instagram will just go really, really quiet. I hope we get to see their real faces. I hope they get to see them too, and realise that actually they're alright without it.

I had a nice day. Nothing happened, nothing didn't happen. It was just a fine day. We baked a terrible apple pie. For some reason I'm not getting my squishy, sugary, gooey bit right. I put chocolate in it, which was a storming success. Then I warmed it up, shoved on a dollop of ice cream and it was YUM. I don't enjoy baking, but the kids LOVE it, so I am going to get better at it. I'll be the next Mary Berry by the end of this. As in, I'll be eighty-five. WHEN WILL THIS END?

I had halloumi for lunch, because now I just fry my cheese.

And here's a really simple salad recipe that I'm thinking of making for dinner, so nice as a side on a hot day:

> Peel and cut an apple into small slices, then halve them
> Chop a shallot (why does that always make me think of Jilly Cooper novels?)
> Chop some celery
> Add some raisins (optional)
> Spoon in a big blob of mayonnaise
> Sprinkle with paprika

It's REALLY yummy. My Aunty Jane used to make it a lot and it reminds me of home. She does the most brilliant BBQs. A variety of meats, lamb steaks, sausages, even some salted mackerel. Her selection of salads was always the best. The one above, with another that always took guests by surprise:

garlic, mint and salt mixed into Greek yogurt, poured lavishly over sliced cucumber. Another would be the freshest Guernsey tomatoes with basil, and then a big bowl of Jersey Royals. We'd sit at the table outside, my uncle in charge of the BBQ, and eat it all up while our tortoise, Daisy, ambled around under the table nibbling our toes. The perfect Sunday, and I miss it so much. It's comforting to imagine them there, carrying on as though things are normal, but without anyone else with them. Daisy will miss my toes, they were always her favourite.

Anyway, any of the salads above go brilliantly with BBQ or ribs. Do you ever do ribs? It's quite American. Ask your butcher for a baby back of ribs. Put the ribs into a shallow baking tray with about half an inch of water. Season the ribs. Wrap them very tight in tin foil and put them in the oven on whatever 200 degrees Celsius is where you live. Cook them for two hours. When done, get them out, SLATHER them in BBQ sauce and put them back in on a higher heat for about fifteen minutes. Until the sauce is all hot and sticky. DONE. BOOSH. BACK OF THE NET – 400 FOOT JIZZ.

Over and out in a storm of food and jizz. How was your day?

Love Dawn x

No Such Thing as Calories in Lockdown

I love food.

I realise that's a basic statement and might not sound like it warrants a whole load of page-time, but for me, it does. Food is the great passion and pleasure of my life. Reading cookbooks, shopping for ingredients, spending hours in the kitchen, making it, serving it and then eating it. Brilliant.

I think my love of food stems from a moment in my childhood where I 'changed' parents. After my mum died, I lived with Nanna and Pop. They were East Enders without a particularly diverse palate. Our dinners were classic 1980s nosh. Findus Crispy Pancakes, ham, egg and chips, fish and chips on Fridays. We'd have a roast on Sundays but, at Pops' request, the meat would be very well done and the veg nice and mushy. I am in no way slamming this menu; I used to think it was the best in the world. My personal favourite (and if you've read my book *Paper Aeroplanes* you will recognise this) was tinned chicken in white wine sauce, with in-the-bag Uncle Ben's rice and lashings of salt. Ideally eaten out of a bowl, on the floor, next to the heating vent in the kitchen. Heaven.

Delicious as it was, there wasn't much in the way of experimentation. Salt and frying made everything delicious. But when I was ten, my sister and I moved in with Aunty Jane and Uncle Tony, and the world of food opened up in a whole new way. All of a sudden, the menu expanded beyond my wildest dreams. Rich and tasty made-from-scratch Bolognese, mussels marinière, fillet steak, grilled skate with capers, avocado mousse (gloriously 1970s, always welcome), and everything served with a side salad, possibly a starter of Parma ham and melon with a drizzle of walnut oil and a selection of good cheese to top it off. My taste buds got the wake-up call of all wake-up calls. I remember at first finding everything a little bland, and my Uncle Tony repeating 'only add salt after tasting', because I was used to a more ready-meal level of saltiness. But I adjusted, and then actual flavours stole the show. My uncle was a pilot and had a little four-seater Piper Arrow plane, G-BAAZ. We used to hop over to various parts of France at the weekends (I know, I know, it wasn't only the culinary part of my life that changed). There is one story my uncle always likes to share about us all being in a restaurant, likely in either St Malo or Dinard. The waiter apparently asked me what I wanted to eat, and I asked for six oysters. Apparently the place went quiet when I proceeded to add, 'And then I'll have twenty-four for my main course.' I was ten. The whole restaurant was struck dumb as they watched this child hoof oyster after oyster, like that was entirely normal.

I have since developed a severe allergy to oysters, coming close to death twice in the space of ten weeks after eating them. The first was raw, the second was cooked, which is why I thought it would be OK. I didn't know that once you have been poisoned by one, you are likely to have the same reaction every time. MY ACTUAL GOD. I won't go into the details of what I went through because it's hands down the most disgusting story imaginable, but put it this way, my oyster days are over. And anytime I see one going towards someone's mouth I turn into the woman from the Shake n' Vac adverts from the 1980s; launching forward in slow motion, screaming 'Nooooooooooo!'

But don't let me put you off if you love them. You eat your oysters. AT YOUR PERIL.

I found the adventure that food offered me one of the most exciting things about life. I experienced loss and true sadness as a kid. Food gave me joy. When I ate, I felt happy. Luckily for me, I am an extremely indulgent person, but I don't have much of an addictive personality. Although there are a few things I should disclaim here in case that statement ever gets contested: I could be on the verge of being clinically addicted to lip balm, crisps, eye shadow and pictures of Cher in the seventies. Apart from that, my indulgences are largely optional. BUT as a teenager my love of food did mean I never particularly loved my body. This was due to two things 1) a massive appetite and 2) no real knowledge of nutrition. Aside from the good food that my aunty cooked me (a pretty solid and varied Mediterranean diet involving lots of fish, olive oil and side salads), when she wasn't looking, the food I ate was terrible. Between the ages of sixteen and eighteen, I averaged about seven bags of Wotsits, two squishy canteen sausage rolls, a blue Boost (that I would separate so I could first eat the biscuit base, and then roll the toffee into a ball), chips and mayonnaise and multiple cans of fizzy drinks EVERY SINGLE DAY. Is it any wonder I never had the confidence to wear a swimsuit on those sunny Guernsey beaches? I used to eat crisps like my life depended on it. I felt uncomfortable in myself. My tummy was always big, my chins followed suit. I wasn't what would be referred to as 'fat' by other kids at the time, but I had a paunch. And I didn't like it. In the nineties, I had no idea that it was the food I was eating that caused it. It's so annoying to look back on it now. I wish I'd just stripped off and run into the sea. I hate how self-conscious I was back then. Such a waste of all that beach time.

Chris and I have been really firm on healthy food, and for that reason the kids get all sorts of treats, but they are always that: treats. We make a real song and dance about every cookie, and Art lights up like Charlie in the chocolate factory when he eats one. I think that's right, for sugar to be a bonus rather than something they take for granted. Also, my kids eat loads of raw vegetables (I'm basically Gwyneth). I picked this up from my sister, who was a few years ahead of me with her boys. I was at her house and saw that she gave them a few chunks of red pepper with their dinner. I didn't think kids ate things like red pepper so was suitably impressed, and I stole this technique as soon as mine had teeth. Art now eats multiple pieces of raw vegetables every night, he chooses to eat them before he eats anything else on his plate. This is because I relentlessly tell them, 'Vegetables help your body make poo.' And as I have two boys, poo is a real hit in this house. Anything that promises it, is a winner. Valentine is more of a meat and potatoes kind of guy. He thinks vegetables are for losers, but I won't give up because I know that one day what they eat won't be down to me, and my nineties diet is not to be repeated.

Regardless of the secret processed food life I was living aged seventeen, I watched and learned from my aunty. Our small island was host to some incredible ingredients. Local beef, dairy, seafood from the rock pools I could see from the end of our garden. She talked about it all like I would new boyfriends. Adoringly, with excitement, with desperation to devour. Aunty Jane set the standard high for me, it just took me a long time to actually live that way myself. As I was launched into being financially self-sufficient at university, my diet got even worse. Disgusting, in fact. With double the amount of alcohol and a heady mix of uppers. But as adulthood kicked in, and especially since I've needed to feed my kids, I see my aunty as my mentor in the way I act about food.

I am a total meat snob. I'm not really into designer handbags, I have a wardrobe full of $20 vintage dresses and my husband and I share a car because we see no reason for the expense of two. We are not overtly lavish in our lifestyle. But meat – that is my financial downfall. There are two reasons for this, the first being animal welfare (you don't have to be vegan or vegetarian to care about how animals are treated). The second is that if I am led to believe there are more hormones in what I am eating than in my own body, I will not enjoy the meal. I think being a meat snob is important for all sorts of reasons, but it is expensive and can, on occasion, make me look like a massive asshole. During the riots, for example (more on those later), Chris called me out for refusing to go to the supermarket closest to us because I didn't like the chicken. 'Dawn, stop being such a massive snob and get the meat from Sprouts!' (A great place for EVERYTHING but meat, in my opinion.) 'I CAN'T HELP IT,' I roared. It's my 'thing'. In my defence, I will buy meat in most places, but I am always looking for the words 'free range', 'organic', 'pasture raised' and most importantly, 'NO HORMONES EVER'.

In lockdown, my meat consumption has gone up dramatically (you might have already clocked this). If this isn't a time to try new recipes and eat like your life depends on it, then when is? Also, as I had agreed with Chris that I would take on the task of all the food shopping and preparing all the meals (my choice, was fun at first, was so over it by June), I've had a lot of work to do. Food has been our greatest joy when being stuck at home, and I've gone for it every day. The one thing that's not quite happened is family mealtimes. Honestly, no. Eating at a table with my kids is too stressful. They get so overwhelmed with excitement that they cannot sit still. Nothing gets eaten, they shout, and Chris and I end up telling them off. No, family mealtimes are a thing for the future.

Our ritual is this, and it will remain this for some time: I give the kids dinner at 5 p.m., then they watch TV while I make ours. We put them to bed around 7.30, then Chris and I kick back, put the telly on and eat whatever I have made with a lovely bottle of wine and we go to bed drunk. PERFECT lockdown evening. Every night. For basically a year. Occasionally losing the wine, so likely drinking double the next night. I suppose I better talk about drinking. Don't worry, that will come, I'll go pour myself a drink and write it.

PIECE FOUR

Drink – Hiccup

4 April
Isolation Update – The bee was on the SOCK

Chris has just handed me the strongest margarita I've ever had in my life, so apologies in advance for any typos in this entry.

Hiccup.

I think my blood is now 100 per cent lime juice.

I refuse to cut back on the booze though, it's the only thing getting me through. As I've said, I'm a pretty indulgent person, but I DO think a lot about what I put into my body. I have a few hard rules that I do break, but only rarely:

1. No processed food
2. No margarine
3. Very little sugar
4. No diet soda or energy drinks
5. No smoking
6. No palm oil
7. No artificial sweeteners
8. None of that fake butter shit they put on popcorn at cinemas, known to me simply as 'cancer juice'
9. No charred meats (unless I burnt it myself by accident)
10. No doughnuts; they are unnecessary and we must have limits
11. Exercise, even if it's just a little bit and despite how much I HATE it
12. And you know how I feel about meat

But as we all know by this stage, I am not perfect. I have my downfalls, and they are:

1. Hot dogs (but only pretentious, organic beef ones that I buy from posh supermarkets and make at home; I would have to be on the floor before I'd eat one from an outlet that couldn't tell me what was in it)
2. Crisps and dips
3. White bread
4. Occasional sweet treats (very occasional, I don't have a sweet tooth)
5. Being polite at a party – if someone invites me into their world and is kind enough to present me with food that consists of any of the above, I will generally abandon all health concerns and happily eat it, because life is for living and gratefulness is key
6. Cheese
7. Fatty meat
8. Pies
9. PASTRY (anything in pastry will have me begging)
10. BOOZE

As my list of downfalls is quite long, I do my very best with the other things to keep my risk of heart disease, obesity and diabetes as low as I can. I'd be able to drop every one of my vices pretty easily, if my health demanded it. But the thing I'd struggle to let go of the most is the booze.

Did I mention I love booze?

So last night, I heard Art scream in the garden. The kind of ear-splitting roar where I immediately presumed we were off to A&E. I was holding a hot roasting dish, and Valentine was next to me, so my response time was slow. Art made it all the way to the kitchen, his face luminous, tears like waterfalls. He couldn't get words out. I scanned his body, but nothing seemed broken, and then I saw it . . . a poor little bee stuck to his sock, stinging him repeatedly with all its goddam might.

I ripped the sock off. A little red dot confirmed it. I wasn't allowed to touch it. Or mention it. Or do anything for quite some time. It felt like Art was blaming me. I mean, sure, I should have sent Valentine out to grind up all the bees with his bare hands before Art went outside. I take full responsibility. I know now.

Poor Art screamed for ages, full throttle. Agony, fear, all of it. I hugged him and thought, 'Fuck me, I'd love a big cry like this.' Kids are so lucky in the way they get to release feelings without judgement. If a grown-up did that, I'd never want to see them again.

Chris took the kids to the park this morning, so I did a thirty-minute Peloton class. It was weird. Usually the Peloton studio is full, and the instructor does a real class surrounded by real people. But today, their studio was empty, and you know what? It made me emotional. I got sad. I had a cry. Not an 'Art bee-sting' level cry, but a little 'WHAT THE HELL IS 2020 TRYING TO DO TO ME' kind of cry. I miss my friend Caroline so much, it's still so raw and it would have been nice to have dealt with it with a more normal life intact. Maybe, I dunno. Grief is shit. Also, I am worried about my aunty, uncle and dad (my three parents). I'm so far from home and can't get to any of them if they get ill. I know I am not alone, so many of us are in this boat. It's shit, and scary and sad. I hope you and yours are doing OK.

But my spin class was good. I did the full thirty minutes, which is unusual as I'm a rotter for dismounting five minutes before the end. I felt *Lizzo voice* – SMUG AS HELL – afterwards. I then had an egg and avocado, but I fried the avocado – and I am telling you it's a thing and you need to do it. That's right, I fry all my vegetables now too.

I'm terrified of running out of crisps, and that's what happened today. All of them, gone. I don't understand where they went. Last time I was in the shop, they were out. I will go to the shops on Monday, and if they are out, well, I guess I will enter a very dark phase of isolation. Also, I check my tequila supply most days. I can generally hold off until late afternoon, but I need to know it's there. By around 10 a.m. I am craving that icy lime flavour of my margaritas. I can only compare it to cigarette cravings when I used to smoke, but I think the fact I don't drink in the mornings means I have the drinking situation under TOTAL control.

Chris and I keep acknowledging we are drinking too much, but then also agreeing these are unprecedented times. We will revert to normal intake when this is over. And if this never ends, then who fucking cares anyway.

I was cuddling Valentine and he pointed at my eye and said, 'Mummy, your eyes are cracked.' He was referring to my wrinkles. You know what? Bog off.

I spoke to my dad. He's so cute and staying home and being an absolute dote. We are talking more than we have in years, and I'm really enjoying it. He makes me giggle. He said he had been sent a really funny Scottish video that made him laugh so much (he is the most Scottish person in Scotland), but that he wasn't going to send it to me because I wouldn't understand it. He then talked me through the whole thing in tiny detail anyway. LOL, dads. I am extremely weepy at the moment. I power through the day but sadness taps on my shoulder constantly. I guess I'm in overdrive, the kids keeping me from collapsing on the floor. But it's always there. Talking to Pops really cheered me up. I miss his amazing cuddles.

I took Potato for a walk this afternoon, and saw a car pull up to a house. Clearly an Uber Eats delivering food. The woman came out of her house and stood really far away from the car, telling the driver he needed to get out and put her food on the grass. I get it, but she was SO rude to him. I glared at her and hoped Potato would wee on her food. SOME people have managed to keep hold of their jobs through all this, and that is wonderful. We should be gorgeous to anyone who is providing any kind of service right now, because they are just trying to keep their lives going, and risking their health so that women like her could have a dumbass vegan stir-fry, or whatever it was she was bossing him around over.

She was dressed in hippie clothes and this is LA, so I am making what I consider to be a fair assumption about her diet.

BE NICE TO PEOPLE. Everyone is struggling. It's all we can do.

You'll all be delighted to know that Valentine wet himself twice, then did a poo on the toilet. So that was all thrilling. I cleared out the Tupperware and baby bottle cupboard. It was a bit sad to get rid of all the bottles, knowing we won't need them again. I always wondered if we might ever talk about a third, but after this . . . FUCK THAT. I am done. Get off.

I made a curry with all the rotten vegetables in the fridge, so I'm really looking forward to getting food poisoning from that.

What else . . . I washed my hair. Fucking incredible feeling. It had been a while.

Love Dawn x

7 April
Isolation Update – What is faster, a . . . OH SHUT UP!

I've been drunk since Friday. I realise that's nothing to show off about. The 4 p.m. margarita has become a crucial element to my day. It's two parts tequila, one part Triple Sec, one part FRESH lime juice. That's my recipe, and that is my drink. I could hoof ten thousand of them in one night (not entirely true). To me, there is nothing more delicious. Safe to say we drank too much and woke up terribly hungover yesterday. At one point I said the words, 'Stop talking to me, I might be sick' to someone. No idea who.

You know when you are feeling anxious so you google the thing to make you feel better? Well I googled, 'What are the drinking stats in Lockdown?' I guess I just wanted to know

I wasn't going to be the only one ordering a new liver on Amazon when all of this is over. This is the result I got:

As you might expect, ***one in five*** *people are drinking more often in lockdown. These people tend to be people who were drinking more heavily and more often to start with. But at the same time, one in three people are drinking less often. And 6 per cent, or more than one in twenty, said that they had stopped drinking specifically for lockdown.*

What the hell does that even mean? One in five are drinking more but one in three are drinking less? I drink too much to understand conflicting stats like that. I took my maths GCSE three times and still never got it, so I'm going to leave the mathematics out of my drinking from now on and just focus on the taste. I am drinking more, yes. As are loads of my friends. I send subtle messages out on WhatsApp like – 'Might have a drink tonight' – to see what kind of response I get, ya know, to make sure I'm not alone.

It's nearly always met with a flurry of drunk responses. Again, this is where the time difference is useful. When I start drinking at 4 p.m. in LA, all of my friends in London are at midnight, already hammered and off to bed. The trick is to only communicate with them when I start drinking early, that way I'm not made to feel bad about it. My friends in LA are drinking more, but they start around dinner time, like normal people. It's best I don't communicate with them until later.

There's loads of chirpy 'YOU'RE ALL GONNA DIE' talk on the radio, and the Prime Minister is in the ICU. It's BANANAS. Everyone is so pissed off with governments, but no one wants that. I hope Boris pulls through, and I hope that it shows people this can happen to anyone, and that being careful is really important. Fucking hell, what a MESS. Los Angeles is going on even more of a lockdown, and the advice is to even stop going to the shops this week if you can avoid it.

I can't avoid it; I have a family to feed. I spent a huge portion of my weekend – when not drunk – trying to find a food delivery service. The earliest delivery I could get was 20 April, almost two weeks away. I don't want to go to the shops, but what the hell else are people supposed to do? The company I found was the ugly veg one, which is great. All the weird-looking produce that the supermarkets won't sell. I'm excited to get some carrots with bollocks and potatoes with nipples. Should give the kids and me something to talk about.

I downloaded *Becoming* by Michelle Obama. I should have read it ages ago but didn't. I'm spending so much time in the kitchen that having a book to listen to, specifically in there, is nice. I tried some fiction, but autobiographies seem to be easier to focus on when both kids are pulling my pants down, begging for snacks. I've done Demi Moore, and now Michelle. Both really good.

On Saturday night we barbecued baby back ribs, sausages and corn. YUM. Valentine spent most of the meal with his arse in the air, yelling 'LOOK AT MY NAKED BUTT.'

I literally have no idea what happened to my life. This is not what I imagined when the plane touched down in Los Angeles nearly twelve years ago. Exactly the opposite, actually. Well, minus the naked arse being in the air, but I always presumed it would be mine.

On Sunday morning, Art woke up early and let Lilu out. Lilu is a Siamese cat and sounds like a screaming baby, so that got me up at 6.30 again. I went into the living room, and Art announced he was going back to bed. Right then, I thought, I'll sit here and contemplate life while the rest of the family sleeps. Great!

Actually, it was nice to be alone. A rare and indulgent treat. We live in a lovely but modest three-bedroom bungalow. Chris and I got this house long before we had kids, and it's perfect in many ways, especially for a couple, but it's a weird shape for a family of four. (It does have a pool though, which is amazing, but it's too cold to go in right now). So we're moving house soon (it was supposed to be last Christmas, it feels like it's never going to happen now) and the new place has an upstairs, which I am so excited about. As things stand, you get to the garden here by walking through our bedroom. This means there is nowhere for Chris and me to escape to. Our bedroom is not a sacred space, there is always someone that isn't us in it. Usually, that's OK, but in lockdown, it's intense. I just hope we get into our new place soon; the idea of being able to close my bedroom door and get some space feels like the dream of all dreams right now. This is why I currently hide in cupboards.

Coming up with activities for the kids is still hard. I had an idea to make macaroni necklaces with them. You paint the macaroni, then thread string through them and make jewellery. Fun, huh? Only, have you ever tried to get string to go around a bend? FUCKING DISASTER. I should have used penne. The lessons you learn, eh?

I give up. TV is better for them than my stupid ideas.

I feel like I didn't stop all day. Also, Valentine pooed his pants on the trampoline. It was so awful. I couldn't cope, so I just threw them away. Oh, and I lay in bed and ate a plate of bacon. Just bacon. On its own. This is not related to the Valentine shitting himself story, I just wanted to let you know that I am now the kind of woman who eats a plate of bacon in bed, like that's normal.

You know what goes well with bacon in bed? Tequila, that's what. Stop judging me, I'll do better when I have an upstairs.

IS IT REALLY ONLY MONDAY?

How you all doing? Tell me the news from your caves.

Love Dawn x

8 April
Isolation Update – Back of the net (who even says that?)

You know you're drinking too much when you have a legitimate breakdown in a supermarket because they have run out of your favourite lime juice. (Funny fact, the lime juice in LA sold out SO fast.) I couldn't believe what I was seeing. Rows and rows of lemon, apple, orange, mango, mango and passionfruit, coconut but no lime juice. WHERE WAS ALL THE LIME JUICE? I walked up and down the aisle like a madwoman, muttering under my mask, 'There must be some here somewhere, THERE MUST BE SOME HERE SOMEWHERE.' I asked a guy who worked there,

'IS THERE ANY LIME JUICE OUT BACK?' He didn't even go to look, he just said no, because it was ALL GONE and he knew it.

WHY IS THE WORLD SO CRUEL?

Instead I got real limes, 450 of them. It's not the same. I mean, it should be. But I find it hard to achieve the perfect level of tartness with real limes, but I will try. Yes I will. BECAUSE I HAVE TO.

I didn't think things would get this bad. But here I am, surrounded by limes but without the perfect juice. Why are they so hard to squeeze? The hardest of all the citrus fruits. THIS is why the lime juice in bottles is so vital. Anyway, I realise the amount I have already talked about this is showing I clearly have a problem.

ONE MORE THING THEN I AM DONE – I am going to buy multiple bottles when it's back in stock, so I am NEVER in this mess again.

OK, OK, I'm over it.

You'll never guess what happened today. I put twenty plastic Easter eggs into a bowl and Art and Valentine threw them across the room. Isn't that FUN?

I've had it with Easter, and it isn't even Easter yet. Knowing that it would be cruel to deprive my kids of chocolate, but also knowing how loopy it sends them, I am nervous about the whole goddam thing. Sunday will be a hard day for us all. The excitement, the treats, the sugar rush, the crash. Be assured I will be drinking by noon.

I did get lamb chops last week though. I'll defrost them Saturday night and do something sensational with them on the big day. I've been thinking about them since I got them. Imagining them in the freezer, hoping they are as succulent as they are in my dreams.

I have spent far too much of my time imagining my lamb chops in the freezer. Please can someone send me some porn?

I had a bad night's sleep. Weird dreams, dark thoughts and I needed a wee but couldn't be bothered to get up to do it.

I ate crisps at 9.30 a.m., 11 a.m., 2 p.m., and 5 p.m. Brilliant. I thought a lot about how I would feel if I ran out again, wondering if I should slow my consumption. But you know what? The world's gone mad, who knows what tomorrow will bring. We have to just eat the bloody crisps.

I'm still so upset about the limes.

Art talks all day long. All day. No breaks. It's pouring down with rain here, so it's quite intense inside with these two children. Sometimes I wonder if Art has a secret speed dealer who slips him drugs under the fence, because he acts like he's off his chops on something . . . all loved up with a LOT of chat. He's like a random fact generator. Dinosaurs, big cats, anything that can run fast, he knows EVERYTHING about ALL OF THEM. It's wonderful, in a way. He watches hours of nature documentaries and retains all the information, but fuck me I wish I could turn him off for twenty minutes. It's really hard to focus on Instagram when he won't shut up.

I got bored today. Actual bored. I kept having moments where I just walked away to sit down. Bored, low energy, couldn't be bothered. Let them throw Easter eggs at the hot oven, they'll work it out. Do you really need to parent constantly to be a good parent? The rain is such a massive kick in the teeth. It makes the days so much longer and harder. The dream would be to light a fire and watch movies all day, but you can't do that with small kids. Art could just about manage it, if I agreed to watch shit all day. But Val gets bored after twenty minutes of TV and wants to play or be occupied in some way. I know this is hard on everyone, but I can't help but wish this had happened when Chris and I first got together. We'd have fucked, eaten and written our way through it. Oh, the books I could be writing . . . maybe lime-squeezing wouldn't be so stressful if I had more time to do it?

But I am not lonely. And I know a lot of people are. I hope you're all OK.

I gave the kids leftover pasta Bolognese for dinner. Valentine ate it like I'd never fed him a meal before, but Art refused. He hates pasta. HATES it. Isn't that the cruellest thing you've ever heard? It means I must try quite hard with their dinners. Which usually I don't mind. But today, I could have served them soil. I just could NOT be bothered.

I had a cheese board with the gooiest cheese at five o'clock, and I didn't touch booze until six. PROGRESS.

I do think I need a few nights of not drinking so my body can have a break. If I never saw another drink again, I wouldn't really care (despite how it may sound in this diary). But I am so enjoying that feeling of, 'And . . . . relax . . .' at the end of the day. Or half-way through the day, sometimes. Usually, I would drink four nights a week, not seven. So, I think I should aim for that. If this is our life now, I have to come out of it with *some* organs.

But what night will I be strong enough NOT to drink? It's food that's the problem. As soon as I taste it, I want wine (post 5 p.m.😉). Tonight, I am making pasta with pesto, bacon and toasted pine nuts for me and Chris – how can you not have red wine with that??

I think we all know what is going to happen.

Oh, Chris came up with a great game to play with the kids in the hallway just before bedtime. He throws as many cuddly toys as he can hold at them, and they must catch as many as they can. Bloody hilarious. I particularly loved it, because while they played, I got to crack open my first bottle of the night.

And that's it from me. It was a long and eventless day.

Love Dawn x

When in Doubt . . . Drink

One friend, who doesn't drink much but also has two boys, just texted: 'Are you drinking every day, or is it just me?' She seemed worried. It was my absolute pleasure to reassure her that yes, I am also drinking every day, despite my feeble attempts not to. She then sent a picture of herself making a cocktail. She looked happy, because this is where we are at.

I live for these texts. The knowledge that alcohol is fuelling parents everywhere, that whatever this new normal is, drinking is a part of it for lots of people. We know (or we hope) it isn't forever. Let's just do whatever it takes to survive and worry about the damage we have done later. That seems like a very grown-up attitude to lockdown, if you ask me.

The thing is, as you may have already fathomed, I love drinking. I love how it tastes and what it does to me. I've never been addicted to it or worry that I could be. I just love it. I am an excellent drinker (these days). I mean, I've been doing it since I was fourteen so I guess I should be. Back in Guernsey in the nineties, we drank to get drunk and for no other reason. Nothing tasted good. We'd somehow acquire cheap wine and down it in someone's bedroom before heading out to, hopefully, kiss some boys. The idea of it makes me feel quite ill now: the cheapest wine, drunk at lightning speed. Actually, that reminds me, we did the same with White Lightning, Diamond White and a revolting cider called 'Brody'. I remember one time hitting up my uncle's drinks cabinet and filling up a bottle with a little bit of everything. I drank it on the cliffs with some boys and we were all sick in front of each other. Sexy times.

Things got a bit more grown-up as time went by, and when we got into pubs and could drink legally we stepped it up. Shots upon shots were a big part of the scene. Sambuca and tequila, Blow Jobs and Slippery Nipples, whatever anyone was buying, I drank. JD and Diet Coke became a staple for me in the later part of the night. But my cousin Charlotte and I would often start with two glasses of white wine with a shot of vodka in each. Not only am I now amazed that we drank this, but I cannot quite believe we were served it. Can you imagine asking for that now and the response you would get? Anyway, Guernsey was a land apart, and growing up there was an absolute honour. Not that I can remember half of it.

I continued to be disgusting into university, where pints upon pints of lager and vodka with Red Bull became the tipples of choice – £1 a pint and £2 for a double vodka and Red Bull felt like all our Christmases came at once. Every day, for three years. My God, how am I still alive? Just thinking of Red Bull now makes me feel sick. These days, I can barely get it past my nose.

When I moved to London it all became a bit more classy. My friends and I started earning a little money, so even though the wine was still gross, and I was a sucker for a 2-for-£10 deal in my local corner shop, it was better than the 3-for-£5 we used to get in Liverpool. By the time I moved to LA when

I was twenty-nine, I'd been wined and dined in some great places, and drinking disgusting wine just to get drunk wasn't something I needed any more. I liked nice wine getting me drunk instead. The drinking scene in LA is different. There isn't such a 'pub culture'. Going for drinks after work isn't a thing for a few reasons. Loads of people are freelance or out of work, or work in production, so there isn't the office culture that demands the same nine-to-five grind. The working day is very different. Also, when I got here, before Uber, you'd have to drive everywhere, so binge-drinking in pubs was a little more complicated as taxis were unreliable and there isn't really public transport. My life in LA has always been about dinners and wine, more than pubs. It suits me better. Nothing gives me more anxiety than drinking with a bunch of people who are not making dinner plans. I need to know I will be sitting down, with no line to the bar, and at least two courses down before 9 p.m. That is all I need from a night out. Despite my love of booze, food wins – always.

Since having kids, I've obviously drunk less, but at the best of times Chris and I are absolutely the kind of people who have a glass (or two) three nights of the week, and more so at the weekends. The rediscovery of tequila has been one of the best things about adulthood. For years, it came in shot form. As a teenager I drank it to the point of blackout more than I can remember. The very thought of it throughout my twenties was impossible because I'd puked so much as a result of it, I couldn't even stomach its name. But then I moved to LA where the Mexican influence is huge. Margaritas with tacos is a common combination here. Friends who had been here for a while would drink neat tequila or have it with soda and lime. I thought this was MADNESS. How could they do that? Why would they be so CHILDISH? But then George Clooney brought out a brand of tequila, Casamigos, and my eyes were finally opened. Someone told me that if all you drink all night is tequila, fresh lime and soda, then you won't get a hangover. Something about the glass of water and vitamin C with every shot. Never one to turn down an opportunity, I tried it. IT WORKED. I mean, I was tired, but I was not hungover. Not in the way I usually was with wine. I was sold. I have since learned that even the sniff of another form of alcohol makes your hangover even worse. It's literally all you can have: tequila, lime, soda. DON'T mess with the system. Going for dinner and having wine, then going on to somewhere else and drinking tequila will cause self-hatred, extreme dehydration and possible regrets the next morning. (That was a good description of one of my hangovers.)

I AM NOT A ROLE MODEL AND DON'T WANT TO BE. DON'T GET MAD AT ME FOR BEING A BAD INFLUENCE, I'M NOT TRYING TO BE A GOOD ONE.

The first few months of the pandemic turned me into a raging alcoholic. Cocktails every afternoon, wine every night. Chris and I went at the whole thing with 'summer holiday' vibes. Knowing it was only 'temporary' and that we had to at least try to party through it. I was also devastated by grief, and the onslaught of childcare and global anxiety took its toll. That late-afternoon margarita became an everyday essential. It was fun, but entirely unsustainable. It was only supposed to be two weeks, wasn't it? Then it was a month. Then it was through to the end of July. And then it was FOREVER. You know when you're drinking too much when you drink too much and don't have a hangover the next day. You also know you're drinking too much when you have a crate of wine delivered on a Wednesday and wonder where it all went on the Sunday. You know you're drinking too much when you buy four bottles of George Clooney tequila and search desperately for the fourth bottle while your husband yells, 'YOU DRANK IT, YOU MORON' behind you.

I am happy to say that, at the time of writing, halfway through 2020, I am back to drinking at a normal level. Maybe even better than that. I'm barely drinking at all during the week. In fact, two nights ago, because I had a small work win, we opened a bottle of white wine and I struggled through two measly glasses. Saying that though, all this talk of booze is making me crave lime, and what is lime without tequila? Here we go again . . .

Here's the thing. I know I can stop if I want to, but I really don't want to. My head is up my bum and my heart is on the ground. Alcohol has been a real highlight of lockdown because it's taken the edge off a lot of pain. Right or wrong, that's how it's been. I say cheers to that.

PIECE FIVE

Strong Eye till I Die

9 April
Isolation Update – Smug as hell

Well the day started triumphantly with a wet bed from Art, a pooey nappy from Valentine, a massive shit in the garden from Potato and a pile of sick from Lilu. Always sets me up for a corker when I basically run the local body fluids removal service.

Why do I even bother showering? There is certainly no point in me doing laundry.

I gave the kids breakfast and stuck the TV on, it was Saturday after all. While they watched nature shows that teach them more than I have ever learned in my life, I thought it might be pleasant to make a homemade face mask. I kept it simple – cucumber and aloe vera gel. I don't have a blender, so I mashed it up the best I could then smeared it on my face. I looked like I had sneezed in a wind tunnel. It was so gross that I washed it off immediately. It gave me visuals of being on the tube and people sneezing on my face. Quite honestly the worst Covid-19-induced isolation visual you could possibly imagine.

I do realise it's not the 1920s and I don't have to make my own face masks, but I am trying to be the kind of woman who makes her own face masks, OK?

One thing I am loving about this is how resourceful I am being with products. By nature, I am a wasteful sod. My sister is the exact opposite. I'd buy new toothpaste long before the old one ran out, for example. In comparison, she would cut the tube in half and keep scraping dregs of toothpaste for weeks. She has a bar of soap, some shampoo and some conditioner by her bath. My bathroom looks like Boots. I have so many products, some that I have bought, some that I have been given (perks of the job). There are half-used bottles of lotions and potions that I've had for years in every drawer. Well, my mission is to buy nothing until I have used them all. Finally, my husband might find a place for his beard trimmer.

Even if it isn't reflected in the unnecessary amount of products I have in my bathroom, I'm reasonably low maintenance when it comes to my beauty regime. I don't get any Botox or anything like that. I get a pedicure now and again and a haircut every three months. I mostly shave rather than getting a wax because I'm not very hairy.

APART FROM MY MASSIVE BUSH.

But lockdown isn't really dragging me away from anything major. The things I do regularly, that I consider to be essential, are:

Scrub my face
Pluck my eyebrows
Spray 7 tons of Elnett into my back-brushed hair
Apply moisture, sunscreen then CC cream
Apply strong eye make-up
Blusher
Straighten my fringe, bobbing it under a little at the end
Moisturise my body
Trim my nails
Take expensive skin supplements called 'Lumity' because what if they really work?

That's kind of it, in terms of the things I do. I can be ready in ten minutes in the morning if I'm not drying my hair.

Maybe I'll start taking long baths and put oils on my hair that would promise phenomenal shine.

But I probably won't, I can't really be bothered.

It'd last for five minutes with the amount of wee and poo everywhere in this madhouse.

ANYWAY. We're going to get takeout tonight, isn't that exciting? Chris wants a Chinese. Yum. Right now, it's 3.30 p.m. and I haven't planned the kids' dinner. The only thing I have defrosted is a tuna steak. Great, I'll cook that and then make a game out of them throwing it back in my face. Maybe if they get it in my mouth, they can have a multivitamin instead of dinner? Perfect.

For lunch I made the boys cream cheese and strawberry sandwiches. Art totally got the concept and loved them, but Valentine acted like I'd handed him a plate of nipples. Honestly, HOW can you not love the idea of strawberries and cream cheese? It's basically a cheesecake sandwich.

I gave them plastic eggs to paint. They made them all look ugly in about three minutes and that was the end of that activity.

I've realised that I haven't exercised in days, and I feel lazy because I'm not moving. The days where I do it are better, no doubt. I'm happier, more energetic and that is SO annoying, isn't it? That exercise is good for you? I wish it was the nineties again, where we really didn't grasp that concept. I ate all those

Wotsits and was quite chunky, but my God I was happy. Now I know too much about nutrition. It's ruined everything. If I could forget one thing that I have learned over the course of my life, it would be that some food is bad for you. What would you like to forget?

Other than coronavirus, obvs.

Love ya,

Dawn x

10 April
Isolation Update – Twit Off, Twit Face

Some bad news. I broke the last of my three favourite hair clips. This is sad on many levels. As you might know, I sport a bob hairstyle, but when it grows a little long, I pin it up into a gentle bouffant style with three extremely specific plastic clips. They are known as 'Octopus clips'. There are thousands of styles, but only one of them works for me. The ones I like look standard but are hard to find. Occasionally, Target has them. Sometimes Boots, but nothing is a given. I buy a few packs when I see them, as they break often. Before lockdown I had three left. I have treasured them since. Regularly screaming 'DON'T TOUCH MY HEAD' at my kids and husband if I feel the clips are in jeopardy. I never, EVER lean back on them when I recline in front of the TV, and I know exactly where they are at all times. ALWAYS out of reach of my boys, who like to pretend they are crocodiles. Today, the last remaining clip refused to clamp. I am bereft.

I, of course, did what I always do when I feel sad and logged on to Amazon to buy things. I scrolled through until I saw them, and made the purchase – but they won't arrive for a week. A WEEK WITH MY SECOND FAVOURITE HAIR CLIPS???

I knew lockdown would get bad, but this?

Today has been going on for weeks. The kids woke up so early and it's torrential rain outside. WHEN will this end?

It was Chris's morning. I was tired. My eyes just didn't want to admit it was morning. Potato had needed to go out in the night, and I struggled to get back to sleep after that. I tried to relax in bed, but for some reason Art was having a massive meltdown, so to the sound of a screaming five-year-old at asshole o'clock, I sipped my coffee in bed.

I missed Twitter today for the first time. I feel out of touch. I'm not doing great at finding my news elsewhere, so end up knowing nothing. In one way, that's nice. I am escaping a lot of drama and anxiety induced by the fear that Twitter instils in people, but I miss being up to date. Chris isn't loving me continuously asking what's going on either, but I have to get my news from somewhere and he always knows everything. You see, I quit Twitter a week before isolation began. I'd been thinking about it for ages, but never thought I'd actually pull the plug. I was in London with my friend Josie (the most beautiful human on earth, a mutual friend of mine and Caroline's). We had just got back from Caroline's funeral and we knew that change had to happen – there was no choice, the best we could do was be in control of at least some of it. We wanted to clean up parts of our lives that were not serving us well. For me, Twitter was a big one. Knowing EVERYTHING about EVERYONE isn't good for us. Why was I seeing stupid comments from right-wing activists who were spreading hate and trying to wind people like me up? Why did I know about the personal lives of loads of celebrities who were telling us too many details of their lives? (She says in her lockdown exposé.)Why could I see one woman tell a male celebrity that she was considering killing herself that night? Why was everyone showing such massive outpourings of love to my friend who just weeks before they had taken great joy in tearing apart? Every time I went on Twitter, I felt like it was one of those flick books of anxiety and stress-inducing comments being rammed into my brain so fast I hardly even noticed, all to come back and haunt me when I tried to go to sleep. It suddenly felt like madness. Who FUCKING cares what everyone is doing? I really don't. It started to feel like I was hiding in people's closets, watching them at their worst through a gap in the door. It's not right. I'm out, for now anyway.

I have no plans to leave Instagram because I think it's a very different platform. You don't get caught up in other people's shit in the same way. You follow who you want to follow and don't see anything else. People don't add you to a conversation where someone is saying they hate you. You're not being fed with opinions that you should have about other people. I realise Instagram comes with its own issues, but in terms of the conversation and for me, personally, it's a healthier and way more fun form of social media. (Also, I love posting pictures of myself looking pretty so I get loads of compliments.)

It's true that Twitter can also be incredible and powerful. My friends Josie, Lliana and I literally launched an entire movement on it. Our charity 'Help Refugees' (now known as 'Choose Love') became the biggest source of aid to the refugee crisis across the globe, JUST from us tweeting about it. It was incredible, electrifying and important. It led me to believe that I needed Twitter to be a good person. I'd post lots of things to encourage people not to be assholes, and then I'd feel good about myself all day. Job done. But it wasn't 'real' good, just flash-in-the-pan good that made me feel good, rather than actually doing any good. We all know that. Tweets won't change the world, but action will.

I do miss the jokes, and the rants, and the news, but I won't give in. I think a lot about how many hours I would lose by being on it right now, and even though I am achieving nothing, I am a lot more present as a result of leaving Twitter. I must stick with it.

Experts are saying we will have to isolate again in the winter, so I've been wondering how to make that easier. With warning and preparation, could this even be fun? The horror of this is that it came out of nowhere and was so new. I mean, it's MENTAL that no one is allowed out because of a virus. Excuse me?

I think we could all get good at isolation, given time to plan properly. How would you do it differently next time? Would you go to your parents? Siblings? Be alone? Get help? Move? Tell me! I'm so tempted by the idea of a babysitter living with us, but the truth is it fills me with fear. Have any of you ever had live-in help? I can't imagine it. It scares me. Or at least it did, until Covid-19. Now I'd let them sleep in my bed. AND with my husband.

I look forward to receiving your applications 😉

I'm making a chicken and mushroom pie tonight. The filling is on the hob now and smells amazing. I had some tarragon so used that. My God, I love pies.

When it rains, the left-hand side of our house sinks and none of the doors work. That's right. I got locked in the bathroom for twenty minutes this morning, and Chris couldn't hear me shouting. I gave up after about four minutes and accepted that I was probably going to live in there forever. It ended up being quite nice. I gave myself great hair and did full make-up. I should get stuck in there more often. Maybe I'll just lock it and pretend that I am.

The only problem was, and brace yourself because this is bad, I was desperate to pluck my eyebrows but the tweezers were in the bedroom. Isn't that awful? I got disproportionately upset about it, then focused on the perfect cat's eye and prayed for no one to find me.

They did. They always bloody do.

I'm still making an effort with my appearance. I can't do the slob thing. I love my clothes and can't bear the idea of not enjoying them. Also, I am emotional about my image and how my boys will remember me. It's not a vanity thing, it's about them having something solid to remember. I am a massive pessimist at heart and always think I'm going to die, isn't that jolly?

Just to really wallow on the sad stuff for a minute, my memories of my mum are all sensory or visual. I was so young when she died, and can't really remember her words, or her voice. But her perfume and eighties sundresses, they're what I think about when I remember her. For me, an image is how you create memories for other people. What do you want them to see when they think of you? And it's not just about beauty, or fashion, or vanity, it's about how you look representing who you are. Which is something that I really care about, personally, and I really work on the connection between my appearance and my soul.

And my soul? Seriously, who the fuck am I?

Anyway, you get my point. Basically, I'm not losing my style during lockdown so my kids will think I'm pretty when they remember me after I am DEAD.

Have I cheered you up yet?

Love Dawn x

NB After I wrote this post I went outside because Valentine was screaming. I found him crouched down, with another bee sting. Art cuddling him, repeating, 'It's OK, Val, it's OK.' My heart melted into a puddle on the floor. Then, having removed the sting, Chris handed me a tequila. It was 4.50 p.m. Everything is going to be OK. I love my people.

Lockdown, but make it Fashion

In many ways, lockdown has challenged our sense of identity and how we look is a big one. When there is no one to make an effort for, do we still make an effort? Personally, I think yes, in some form or another. Because our lives essentially become other people's memories, and it starts with how you look.

Some people say they don't care about that stuff, and I think that's totally fair and wonderful, but it also tells their story as much as someone who does. Whether you wear designer Hermès scarves around your neck on a casual day, or 3-for-$20 cargo shorts from a catalogue, you are telling us about you with your clothes. You are creating your image. We are getting to know you before you've even said a word.

It doesn't mean those who have no real care for putting outfits together are not interesting, creative and vibrant, like 'fashion' makes us believe people are. It just means they have more important things to think about, as far as they are concerned, which is a massive statement on their character and one that we can all admire. If I spent less time worrying about this stuff, I'd write approximately six more books a year.

But I spend a lot of time thinking about the way I look. I always have – not that I've always got it right. As a teenager on Guernsey, the safest thing was to follow trends and fit in, but I always hated nineties clothes, even in the nineties. I would occasionally try to go rogue, and I'd throw together something that I thought might make some waves in my social group. One look was a giant, oversized mustard turtleneck jumper with GREEN JEANS and purple DM boots. I thought my use of colour was admirable, but I got called many things that day ('giant banana' and 'pot of Colman's' being two of them). I later went through a phase of wearing baby blue flares that didn't really fit, with varying T-shirts that had funny slogans on them. This became my look for most of my sixth form, when I started to work in a pub. My favourite was one that said 'SIZE IS EVERYTHING' in big bold letters. I'm so glad smartphones didn't exist back then, as I can keep any physical photographic evidence of these fashion nightmares locked safely and securely away.

But I tried, because I knew I cared about clothes. I knew they weren't just things that I wore, and I knew fashion trends were not for me. I didn't want to look like everyone else, but I had no idea how to style myself back then, I was looking in the wrong places. Fashion mags were full of really well put together people, but that isn't me. I dress emotionally. I know that sounds wack, but it's true. The reason I love vintage is because the clothes that I buy make my tummy flip when I find them. I'm like the kid in *The Goonies* when he finds One-Eyed Willy on the ship. The way his eyes light up at the shiny gems, that's me in a vintage shop. The entire process thrills me. The effort of rooting through so many things, only one of each, waiting to spot something that attracts me. Then, the anticipation of it fitting, then the sheer joy when it does. I love spending my money on things I know no one else has. I love knowing there are not multiples of that piece in different sizes. People say to me 'how did you find that dress?' and I love to tell them 'I didn't, it found me.' I don't care if a dress costs $10 or $500, I can love them just as much. When I realised my 'style' was a feeling rather than a look, everything came together.

There were no vintage shops in Guernsey when I was growing up, so I couldn't have known what was to come. Years before discovering vintage I'd started to veer towards those shapes: sixties-inspired tops, and eighties party dresses. But they were all remakes, and something about them never gave me a thrill, but I was heading in the right direction. My aunt and uncle were furriers in sixties London (don't get cross, they don't do it now and I do not support the fur trade on any level), and as a result they were very passionate about the way clothes were made. As they had largely made bespoke pieces to order, I think they drummed it into me how much a piece of clothing can mean to someone, and what goes into making them. It took me a while to work out my place in fashion, or my version of it. But my clothes and the effort I put into my appearance are a big part of who I am.

I dream about dresses and design them in my head all the time. For fun, even when I'm not shopping, I trawl Etsy and eBay. The first thing I do when I buy a garment is turn it inside out to see how it was made. Sometimes, they were made by designers, other times you can tell that a woman likely made it herself following a pattern, and those are my favourites. I love the history of clothes, how different styles defined the decades. But I also love the clothes' own personal history. Nothing gets me going more than when someone can tell me who a garment belonged to. My wedding dress, for example. I got it from my dear friend William Banks-Blaney who is the genius behind 'William Vintage', which was a very high-end shop in Marylebone, selling exquisite Dior gowns and Chanel suits likely stitched by the lady herself. I knew I wanted to wear vintage on my wedding day, so went straight to him. We'd been playing around with a gorgeous, almost golden Dior gown. It came with all of the internal corseting and was truly the most stunning, elegant and photogenic dress. BUT, it was very formal. That wasn't the kind of bride I wanted to be and the fact that I had committed to it, and a seamstress was working to make it fit, was keeping me up at night. For one fitting I turned up and I was notably morose, but would never have admitted why. William put the dress on me and I agreed, it looked gorgeous. But it wasn't right. It was expensive. And I felt like I'd made a massive mistake. And then, as if a magical spell had been cast over me, my eyes were drawn to a heap of twinkling blue tulle that was slumped onto a chair.

'What is that?' I asked William.

'Oh, I need to steam it. It's a gown that belonged to Princess Lillian of Belgium, I—'

I stopped listening. As I walked over to it, I tossed aside the Dior. I picked up Lillian's dress and stepped into it. My reaction? I couldn't stop dancing.

'This is the bride I want to be,' I told William. And because he is wonderful, he agreed. The Dior went back on the rail, and Princess Lillian's blue dress, which fitted me perfectly, became the dress I got married in. I was so proud of its history.

Dresses make me disproportionately happier than any

material object should, and just because I wasn't allowed to leave the house during lockdown, I never gave up on my outfits. Kaftans, jumpsuits and novelty skirts got me through it. And when I say they got me through it, I mean they made me feel happy. Clothes do that for me. I don't know if that makes me kooky or shallow, but it's how it is. I do think it probably stems from being a writer and having worked in a solitary way for many years now. I learned pretty early on that if I didn't get dressed in something I loved, I wouldn't get much done.

As some people may reach for jeans, the outfit I reached for most on a day in lockdown was a voluminous, high-waisted, green striped skirt with watermelons all over it. I wear it with a cut-off green-and-white-striped T-shirt (it clashes, and I love it) that I got in a clothing swap at my workspace. I've had the skirt for over ten years. It came into my life when my friend Ophelia had been living in my flat while I was away, and she left it there. When I got home and found it, I loved it so much that I didn't mention it to her. I agreed with myself that she had six months to claim it before I took it for my own. She never did. To this day, she has never mentioned this sensational skirt, which means it meant nothing to her, which literally makes no sense to me because it deserves better. Ophelia, if you're reading this, I know we never discussed this out loud and I am sorry for that. You are one of the most stylish people I have ever met, but you really lost me on this one, girl.

The skirt became my lockdown uniform. Teaching me that comfortable clothes can still be awesome, and as I create these childhood memories for my kids, they will remember me in colours and print. Hopefully this will make them feel as happy to look back on as they made me feel at the time.

I know most people didn't bother with 'outfits' during lockdown, and I get that too. A lot of my friends said they spent most of their time on Zoom calls dressed like news readers. Smart up top with PJs on the bottom. I probably did five Zoom calls throughout the whole of lockdown – luckily that isn't my world and the social ones never worked because of the time difference with LA. But I'd like to assure you that even for those five, my outfits were awesome.

If you think I am being ridiculous, I'm not. Think back to your childhood. Was it your mother, your dad, a teacher or a friend's mum whose image you can see as clear as day even now? That's because something about it became an emotional memory for you. I have a few. As I mentioned, I remember very little of my mum, but the smell of her Chanel No. 5, the creaking of her black leather trousers, the silk of her eighties party dresses – I'll always remember those. I may not know what she sounded like, but I can see her, smell her and feel her whenever I need to. I want my kids to be able to see, smell (Dior Addict – it's the one Charlize Theron advertises; I know, I know, the similarities between us are endless) and feel me for the rest of their lives too. And so I work on those things for them, even in lockdown, because one day I'll just be a memory. And I want that memory to be awesome.

Also, I hope that by me wearing great clothes they will choose girlfriends (if they veer that way) who wear awesome things that I can borrow. I also need someone stylish to leave all of my clothes to, and I am on a genuine mission to work out who that will be.

Good clothes make me feel happy, so whether anyone sees me or not, I keep wearing them. I do wonder though, if there will be people out there who might take this as an opportunity to re-emerge as something different. Maybe their style has always bored them, or they felt too self-conscious to try anything new. But life will never be the same after this because we've all lived through the unimaginable, so if this isn't an opportunity to fire up some new looks when you're allowed to step outside your front door again, I don't know what is. Change has been forced upon us, so why set limits on how much of it we can take for ourselves? Isn't that a lovely thought? When the world experiences such change, maybe individuals can get on the bandwagon.

PIECE SIX

Raising Boys

11 April
Isolation Update – Get back in the kitchen, bitch

All I do is laundry. Mountains of it. I want to do less, but my kids are disgusting and everything is either covered in sauce or wee, so I have no choice. But I am SO bored of folding small clothes. SO bored of it. And WHOSE idea was it for socks to match? Seriously? That person HATED women.

This morning, after I had given the kids breakfast, Valentine couldn't find me. 'Mummy, Mummy, where are you?' he yelled as he tore around the house. Chris was taking over, so I remained in my bathroom where I was putting on my pointless make-up for the day. After quite a few minutes, I couldn't ignore it any more. I had to ask him what he wanted.

'What, Valentine, what?' I barked, only one eye done.

'Why aren't you in the kitchen?' he said, quite cross.

'Because I am in the bathroom.'

'No, Mummy. You get back in the kitchen.'

'No, I'm here now.'

'You have to STAY IN THE KITCHEN.'

Right, so raising boys who don't see women as domestic servants is going about as well as Covid-19.

I made a sensational chicken pie last night (just to prove that my place IS in fact in the kitchen). I made quite a big one, so dinner tonight would be sorted. We ate it all. Just Chris and me, all of it. Whoops. Sausages tonight! I always have a back-up plan.

Valentine woke up with a massive foot. My poor baby. He'd woken in the night, Chris went in and he was happy with just a cuddle. So Chris didn't see the foot at first. My God. Guys, it was like a balloon. The skin was going to pop. It was around the bee sting he got a few days ago. It was absolutely some kind of reaction so I gave him some Benadryl and left a message for the doctor, just to be sure. She called, I did everything right, and Ole 'Chubby Toes' is doing fine. It's still huge, but doesn't seem to be bothering him. Which is good, because this morning I panicked and presumed he'd lose the foot. I have a tendency to do that.

Did someone say CORONAVIRUS?

I had to google what day it was because I couldn't even hazard a guess. Was happy to hear it's Friday: the kids watch loads more TV at the weekend and I get even more drunk and high. I wish it was the weekend every day. Oh no, wait . . .

The summer term starts here again on Monday. I have the fear.

I've quite enjoyed the chaos of the past few weeks. We have our schedule, but we can do what we want. It's been OK, I could do this for a while. But I can tell Art needs more stimulation, so I get it, school is good. I just get scared because I found school terrorising the first time round, and I feel like this is going to be harder for me than Art.

GET OVER IT, DAWN, HE ONLY LEARNS ONE LETTER A WEEK.

OK, OK, I'm fine.

Valentine hasn't wet himself for a few days. I do believe we've done it.

I made him a den in his old cot. The duvet fell down. He said, 'THIS DEN IS NOT GOOD ENOUGH.' He's two. This is not right. Isn't he supposed to be cuddling me all the time and being cute? Why does that bit pass so quickly?

I made them a cheese and salami quesadilla for lunch. Art ate it all, Valentine picked out the salami and dropped the rest on the floor. Should I just feed him spaghetti hoops until he is old enough to cook for himself?

I did a Peloton. The instructor was from London and she made me homesick. The good thing about being homesick at the moment is that it's totally pointless because, even if I was at home, I couldn't see anyone anyway. So there is that. But still, I miss the London streets and being in the same time zone as my people.

I made a leek and potato gratin, but I put sour cream in the milk and the damn thing curdled. I am DEVASTATED, I really worked at it. I might have to drain all of the liquid off. Weird. But I don't want Chris to notice because it tastes amazing and he doesn't need to know about the UNSIGHTLY curdling.

Is that me being a good wife, or a terrible wife? It's hard to know sometimes, isn't it?

Well, it's just gone 4 p.m. Chris just handed me a tequila and I acted all, 'I wouldn't drink that now' then took it gently from his hand and it's almost gone. But hey, according to Google, it's Friday.

Have a lovely weekend, you gorgeous humans. I hope you managed to get enough chocolate delivered. I got the boys a chocolate bunny each, and about an hour ago Art said, 'I hope I don't get a silly bunny for Easter.'

Oh, the joys!

Love to you all . . . and HAPPY EASTER!

Love Dawn x

14 April
Isolation Update – Who ate the Easter Bunny?

We got through Easter weekend because we drank. That's how.

So it's important for me to tell you that I am extremely hungover. Chris and I decided to up the tempo after the kids went down last night. We got exceptionally high and sang karaoke in the living room until 1 a.m. We laughed so hard we cried. We needed it. The last few months have been intense in many ways, we needed a blowout. So, we did. We really, really did.

My friends Louis and Nancy got me the karaoke set for my birthday last year (I've never felt so seen), and Chris has hooked it up to the TV in the living room. The remote is now voice-controlled, so all I need to say is 'Show me Dolly Parton "9 to 5" on YouTube Karaoke,' and then I can get on with living my best life.

I must admit though, it's really weird doing karaoke now. It's always been my favourite thing. But it was also something that I did with Caroline. We sang all the time. So many people at her funeral talked about her love of it, and now, I cannot deny that it's changed. I could feel the tears coming a few times but I just kept telling myself to turn it into joy. To imagine her there, singing her heart out, having the time of her life. Singing was her passion, she was so good at it. As I chose songs last night, I couldn't believe how many reminded me of her. We have so many memories. One in particular was 'Jolene' by Dolly Parton. I celebrated my fortieth birthday in Margate last year and I sang with a band. Caroline couldn't come because she was working, but managed to get out early in the end and got a cab all the way from London at about 9 p.m. to surprise me. I was so happy. She always showed up for me. Always. As I sang, she was right there at the front singing along with me, dancing her cute dances. The best audience member ever. After I did 'Jolene', she came over, hugged me and said, 'That is your song.'

No baby, now it's 'our' song.

Even Dolly Parton reminds me of her.

Art is asking if I would be willing to change his name to 'Speedy'. I've asked him if we can find something cooler, like 'Shot' or 'Cheetah', but he is insisting on 'Speedy'. I told him it sounds like a joke name for a tortoise, to which he said, 'But that's not funny, because tortoises aren't fast.'

Do you ever feel like you're just talking to the walls?

The upsetting thing is that I love the name Art. I got pregnant in New York, when Chris was doing *Of Mice and Men* on Broadway. Chris was about four stone heavier than he is now, with a huge, long beard and a shaved head (it was for the part). I still had sex with him though. And then, on a toilet in a weird apartment just below Park Slope, with Lilu and Potato sitting at my feet, and possibly one of the worst hangovers imaginable, I peed on a stick and found out that we were going to have our first baby.

I'd always loved the name Art. Chris did too. But it was very late one night back in 2014 that we knew for sure that would be his name.

I'd been to see my friend Neil Gaiman, who was doing a book reading at Carnegie Hall in New York. He invited us to the after-party, and Chris came to meet me there after the show. The party was in someone's loft apartment in Soho. It was an old school, arty crowd. Native New Yorkers with the kinds of jobs you'd read about in sexy sixties novels. There was the picture editor of the *New Yorker*, artists, actors, poets and designers. I loved it. I felt like it was as close to being a part of the seventies New York Art scene as I could get. And then, as I was really starting to fit in, Neil said 'Dawn, Chris, I have to introduce you to the coolest man in the world.'

That man was called Art Spiegelman. A renowned political cartoonist as charming as he is wonderful. Neil was right, he's seriously cool. I was only a few months pregnant, so keeping it quiet, but we'd been talking about the name Art a lot, so got a sharp thrill when we met this amazing man. We knew there and then that, if the baby were a boy, Art would be his name. And so it came to pass. And no, every news outlet that ever mentions my kids, his name is not Arthur. We never said the name Arthur, but for some reason, you insist that it is. It isn't, his name is just Art. Art O'Porter. The coolest guy that ever lived. (Sorry, Mr Spiegleman, you've been outdone.)

So you can see why it's annoying that Art wants to change his name to the 100 per cent less cool 'Speedy'. But in these testing times, I'll call him whatever it takes to stop him tugging at my clothes and allow me to drink my tequila in peace.

I felt sad and homesick at the weekend. I'm not religious, but I would always have people over on Easter Sunday. I'd cook too much, drink too much. I also missed Caroline crazy amounts, because I thought of her eating a big Sunday roast and drinking lashings of red wine with her family in a pub. And it made me cross and sad that she wouldn't be doing that. I kept expecting her to text. I often read back her texts, stalk her Instagram, listen to a podcast we did together, and she still feels so alive. How does someone like that just disappear? I still have no idea what happened, I know it will take years to understand. I also know that I might never. I love her so much.

The Easter bunny came on Saturday night, and deposited forty-eight plastic eggs stuffed with candy all around the house and garden. I left a chocolate bunny and a little card with a balloon on it on the dining table too. When the kids woke up, they were so happy, and my cockles warmed right up. They ate chocolate for breakfast, then did their Easter Egg hunt and loved every second. Then we all had eggs and bacon, and at 5 p.m. we had the most amazing lamb chops with all the classic roast sides. As usual, the novelty of us eating with them sent them into a frenzy, and Valentine lay on the floor rubbing the lamb chop on his face, Potato looking on, wondering when I would turn away so he could lick it off.

Speaking of Valentine, he is officially potty trained. What a mission that was, but it's done. No accidents in three days. My house will always have a lingering smell of piss, but no more shitty trousers. Thank GOD. Thanks for being here for me during that dark time.

I'm really enjoying *Becoming* by Michelle Obama. The way she talks about Barack when they got together is dreamy. HE SMOKED!!! I can't get my head around that. She also described him as a 'unicorn' and 'other worldly'. Isn't that glorious? She said he never had any real interest in owning anything, that he genuinely cared about society and he was so well read that he'd stay up every night, into the early hours, just reading and reading. Books about American history, fiction, all of it. Just a charming, kind, clever, educated, classy as fuck guy. Compare that to the orange twat we're dealing with now and have a nice big cry on behalf of America.

WHAT IS HAPPENING.

I'm very happy with my new 'kitchen book' scheme. I have one audiobook that I only listen to in the kitchen. As I seem to be in the kitchen twenty-two hours a day right now (it's my choice, just to be clear; I insist on it because, as much as I moan, it's my happy place), I'm getting through them at a hefty speed. I find reading hard because I am always so tired by the time I get to bed, but my goodness, I love a good audiobook.

Art's school started today, so we had to check in with his class on Zoom. Just what I needed after my first big night in months. It's SO hard, he finds it so boring. I'm gutted for him because he loves his mates and loves school. And weirdly, he's perfectly happy in isolation, until he is reminded of what he's missing out on.

Also, it makes me sad that he's on a screen. He's never even had an iPad. I was excited to hold off the digital side of things for as long as possible, because he'll spend a lifetime on a computer and phone when he starts. And it made me sad this morning, to see him sitting there like it was his job and he was at work.

But I know this is what it is, and that he does need to stay connected to his class and teachers. Still, it's so far from ideal for a very active five-year-old. I'm sure any of you who are parents feel the same way.

Going to bed was funny. Chris had to kick the bathroom door in again, so I could get out, and he saw the handful of pills I was taking. For a moment I think he was worried. 'What the hell are you taking?' he asked, like I had a hand full of uppers and downers. My answer was literally the most un-rock-and-roll ever: 'Ten milligrams of melatonin, some skincare supplements and an Advil.' Oooooooo, hardcore.

This made us laugh. Laughing feels good.

So that was that. A nice Easter with the kids, and a fun party night with my husband. It led to the kind of hangover that nearly broke us both, but it was totes worth it to feel like grown-ups.

OK, it's 6.30 p. m. I need to bath these monsters and then bath myself. Make today stop, it was hard.

Love Dawn x

15 April
Isolation Update – I'll spatchCOCK your chicken in a minute!

Just a quick one tonight, the sofa is screaming my name. I need to dunk some spatchCOCKed (am I twelve?) chicken into some panko crumbs, fry them, pour wine, and then we're going to watch *Jaws 2*. Big night!

Oh man, today was a better day. All I remember from yesterday is wandering around my house on all fours, begging for the day to end. After a lot of begging, it ended. I slept. All was well, and today was good. In fact, and I know this is weird, I quite enjoyed it. Even though NOTHING happened.

This afternoon, Valentine walked into the kitchen with an entire loo roll wrapped around him. I don't know how he did it, but I ran at him in super slow-mo 'DOOONNN"TTTT YOOOUUU KKKNNNOOOOWWW HOOOOWWW PREEECCCCSIOUUUS TTTHHHAAAT ISSSSS?'

Of course he bloody doesn't. He's two, and only started using the stuff last week.

I got a funky face mask that I wore to the shop, but it really scratched my nose. How did I come out of the supermarket with a nose injury, when I did everything right? URGH. Also, when I was paying, my dress got stuck between my bum cheeks, but I was holding something so I couldn't get it out. I turned around to see if anyone saw, but they all had face masks on so I couldn't tell if they were laughing or not. GUYS, how will we know if people are judging us if they are all wearing face masks?

As if life wasn't hard enough.

OK, I have so much more to say but I must bread the chicken for dinner, so more tomorrow. I am SO hungry and need wine.

Love you,

Dawn x

16 April
Isolation Update – My kids are pink

We woke up this morning to hear the kids playing, which was delightful. Then they asked Alexa to do a 'Farty Party' so we had to wake to ten minutes' worth of constant fart sounds. Always a lovely start to the day. But it was my morning off, so I lay in bed like a lush drinking coffee, then got up and did full make-up just in case Instagram inspiration should strike. It didn't today. Sometimes I can't stop, other days I have nothing.

I feel like things are getting more positive, don't you? I realise we are not out of the woods and there are still thousands of cases and many more deaths that we will endure, but the tone here has changed. When I got back from London a month ago, people were buying guns and talking about the army commanding the streets outside our homes. It felt like we were heading to war. But it doesn't feel like that any more, or at least, it certainly doesn't feel like things will get worse.

We'll be isolated for a long time though, that's for sure. Normal life is a while away, and who knows what our new normal will be. Ten people at a time in a restaurant? Having our temperatures taken before we get in an Uber? Dating with face masks on? Kinky. Maybe.

It was hot today, and finally the pool was warm enough to go in, so the boys splashed around all day. It was nice, I felt like we were on holiday and feel very grateful that we have it. Art has got really good at swimming, and Val just hangs on the steps with his floaties on. But he loves washing all his sea creatures and then throwing them in my shoes (the sod). I swam up and down for ages, and now I can't move my arms. Also, I forgot about sunscreen and both the kids are quite badly burnt. I'm not looking forward to the inevitable lack of sleep they will endure as a consequence of my negligence. MUM FAIL.

We had hot dogs for lunch. I had one too. SO GOOD. A pretentious, organic beef hotdog in a brioche bun. Drenched in mustard and ketchup with a side of crisps and a random mango, because it was going off. Perfect.

I decided to get in the bath with the kids tonight, trying to scrub off all the aloe vera I had to slather on them to mitigate the burn. It was fun, they loved it. At one point, Art's foot accidentally touched my vagina and he thought it was hilarious. I do my best to be very open with my body in front of them, no shame, nothing to hide, nothing to make fun of or be uncomfortable around. But when your five-year-old accidentally shoves his foot up your fanny you have to scream, 'DON'T TOUCH THAT!' Don't you? I mean, it was a bit of a knee-jerk reaction, to be honest, because I thought he'd done it on purpose, and as a feminist mother rule number one is: make sure your son knows that sticking his foot up a woman's vagina without her approval is not OK. I'm sure my reaction has put him off forever. Imagine that? What was supposed to be a nice family bath, now the catalyst for a lifetime fear of vaginas. Damn it.

Tonight, I am making a sticky pork stir-fry from Jamie Oliver's *Five Ingredients* book. Which is the perfect cookbook for a lockdown. And of course, we will watch *Jaws 3*. I bet I can guess what happens.

Sending you all the love in the world.

Love Dawn x

17 April
Isolation Update – Can I licky your dicky? (You 'eard.)

I wore my watermelon skirt today. I love it because it has an elasticated waist and none of my clothes fit me because a) all I do is eat, and b) all I do is drink, and c) I always have the munchies. But Valentine KEPT pulling it down, revealing my terrible and massive Marks and Spencer's knickers that are so awful I don't even want my kids to see them.

Being a feminist mother of boys is hard. I screamed 'YOU DO NOT PULL DOWN A WOMAN'S SKIRT . . . UNLESS SHE ASKS YOU TO.' I added the last bit because, as much as I want to raise my kids to respect women, I also want them to know that some women are totally up for it and find the element of surprise thrilling. It is SO hard to get it right.

Lockdown has often made me wonder what the day-to-day nonsense would be like with daughters. But then I think back to the way my sister and I used to fight. I'd take dinosaur facts on a loop over that any day, I reckon. I love being a mum to boys – and I have to admit, mine are really good ones.

In other news, I butchered some cupcakes today. WHY am I so bad at baking? I also made some sausage rolls which were pretty good. And I ate loads of crisps and started drinking at 4 p.m. All in all, a pretty successful day.

We had a very exciting morning. Potato ran outside and started barking, which is unusual because he doesn't say much. He does shout at squirrels, but this was full-on. I went out, and OH MY GOD, guys . . . it was the most amazing thing. Alongside the pool, past the fence and sort of trapped, there was an opossum (or is that an O'possum, when it's at our house?). She was HUGE, like the size of a big cat. I'd have leapt a thousand feet into the air if I didn't already know that these guys are really sweet. A tiny one (probably the same one) had been on our porch about a year ago, and Lilu had it cornered. I freaked, but then researched them to discover they are not aggressive AND they eat cockroaches. This was excellent information, as we had an infestation at that time and I was losing my mind. I went out, picked Lilu up and told the O'possum (let's run with it) she could stay if she ate all the critters. She said she would and ran off.

A week later, and by total chance, one of Art's friends had her birthday party at the zoo and one of the zookeepers came over holding an O'possum for us all to stroke. It was awesome, because we could ask loads of questions and get prepared for seeing our new housemate again, but we never did. I do, however, hear things running around in the roof sometimes. It's usually either racoons or these guys; now I'm pretty sure that little one we saw is now the big one we saw today, and that SHE has been here the whole time.

What happened next was magical.

I called Chris and the boys. Art and Valentine are obsessed with wild animals, so you can imagine how excited they were. Then Chris went all gooey and said, 'Oh my God, look at her back.' I'm quite blind and it looked to me like she had a really messed-up coat, but then we realised she had SIX BABIES on her back. Guys . . . oh guys . . . Oh God it was so beautiful. O'possums are marsupials ('THAT IS NOT A KANGAROO,' said Art). They carry babies in pouches. These babies were all hanging on to her back in the most perfect orderly way. I almost cried. We told her she was so welcome and called her 'Opsie'.

Remember the worms that Chris ordered a few weeks ago? Well, we put them on the side of the pool where we saw her. That is a much more natural demise for them than at the hand of my monster baby, Valentine.

Then I worried. I had to have this place covered in gel poison because of the cockroaches. They take it back to the nest and it kills them all. After years of using spray and them returning over and over again, this finally worked. When I saw the O'possum I thought, what if she finds the nest and eats the roaches, and gets poisoned?? But wanna know something amazing about O'possums? They are immune to poison. Isn't that fantastic??

So it's all worked out really well. She can stay. She can kill all the bugs. And I can raise her babies as my own, as if we are sister-wives. What a dreamy plan.

I gave the kids chicken on sticks for lunch. I buy them in the supermarket. Just chicken, on sticks. Pretty simple, but they love them. I will make them myself when I'm not too busy ruining cakes. Anyway, as I was serving them, I started singing a song 'Chicken on sticks, sticks, sticks. Sticky sticky chicky chicky.' But then it progressed to 'Licky licky chicky. Chicky dicky, licky licky dicky licky.' I was basically dancing around the dining table singing about licking dicks.

I stopped, of course, then Art yelled 'LET ME LICKY YOUR DICKY' across the room.

I put the news on loudly and pretended I couldn't hear him. Then had to hide in the pantry to laugh.

OK, tonight is homemade sausage rolls with salad. I hope you're all OK.

Love Dawn x

PS My sausage rolls are SO easy if you want to make them. I think it's an old Jamie Oliver recipe. Here's how it goes:

1lb sausage meat (pork mince)
1 finely chopped shallot
Some chopped-up sage . . . I use about 7 leaves
Salt and pepper
One sheet of pre-rolled puff pastry

In a bowl mix the meat, shallot, sage, salt and pepper.

Roll out the pastry, cut into two long oblongs. Place a long sausage (OO-ER) shaped wedge of the meat mix down the centre of each one, then fold the pastry over the top, helping it stick with egg. Paint all the pastry with egg. Stick in oven. Get them out when cooked. Give them to your lover and enjoy getting some action.

NIGHT, KIDS,

Love Dawn x

The Perfect Men

I am determined to be an embarrassing mother. I have a fantasy in my head of going into the boys' room when they are about fourteen and sixteen and explaining to them how they must be with girls and saying some unthinkable things that mothers probably shouldn't say. But maybe if mothers DID say them, they would stay in the kids' minds forever, and shape them into the perfect men? My boys will be big, confident and loud, because that is who their parents are, and our job is to make sure that, because of that, they don't act like assholes. It all starts here.

It's hard to find the balance of wanting to make them respect women and be mindful of what they say and do, but also be relaxed and have loads of fun. My fear of my sons ever making a woman feel uncomfortable with their behaviour is terrifying. When I was a teenage girl, numerous teenage boys behaved in ways that would be unacceptable now. A big reason for this is that the parameters were never laid out for them. No mother had ever said 'sex isn't all about you, it's about her too.' So, they came at us girls with their big teenage erections, tongues hanging out of their mouths and ready to penetrate whatever hole was available first. I remember one time passing out at a party (I would have been around fifteen, we started young on Guernsey and I was always classy) and waking up to a boy's hand in my knickers. It was so random. I had never even flirted with him, he came out of nowhere, saw a sleeping girl and tried his luck. When I woke up, I told him to go away and rolled over. He wasn't very nice to me after that. He's a forty-something-year-old man now, married with kids. I saw him walking down the street in Guernsey a few years ago and I think he said, 'hi'. Does he remember that night and feel weird about it, or is that a memory that blurs into all of his teenage sexual adventures, because for him nothing actually happened? Probably. He didn't get to have sex with me when I woke up, so that was that. But it stayed with me forever. I don't want my boys to be bad memories that stay with women forever. The originators for stories that thirty years later they mention in books, because they realise they've never said it out loud and it actually really bothers them.

So, I plan to have those conversations with my sons, so they know the parameters of what is and what isn't OK. My belief is, if they ever find themselves tempted to do the unthinkable, they will hear their mother's voice saying, 'Don't you dare!' and stop. This is a job that I think I can do, I think I can train them well. But on the other hand, I want them to be spontaneous and fun. I want them to feel safe in themselves, to enjoy sex and be giving and generous. I want them to be wonderful lovers (this is getting SO awkward), and respect women. But I also want them to be secure enough in themselves not to be trampled all over. Because, as I know myself from being one, girls can also be total assholes.

The chat I plan to have with them one day, goes something like this.

- Never try to finger a girl under a blanket in a room full of people because you think you can get away with it.
- Always wash your willy before a blow job but never tell her your mother told you to do that. In fact, never mention me during sex. Ever.
- If you are being sexual and she seems unsure, stop. If things get saucy for a second time, and she seems unsure again, ask her what she would like and encourage her to be honest with you. Tell her it only turns you on if it turns her on, so to guide you in what she would feel OK with. If she still seems unsure, just stop.
- If she's slept with more people than you and it bothers you, that's your problem, not hers. Don't make her feel slutty to make you feel like more of a man. You won't look more like a man, you'll just look like an asshole.
- If she is ravishing you and you're not into it, be careful how you handle that. Your insecurity in bed doesn't mean your ego needs to make her feel bad. It's OK for her to be into stuff that you're not into, it's not a reflection on you. Send her on her way with confidence and no humiliation; by doing that you will help her find someone who likes what she wants. Sexual compatibility is important. Neither of you should try to be someone that you are not in bed. Also, if she makes you feel silly or is rude about your

technique, body or penis, then leave. Come home and tell Mummy, and I'll go duff her up for you.

- Never act like what you are into is more important than what she is into. Ask her questions and listen to her answers. You can make it clear what you like, just be nice about it. If she isn't nice about what she likes and makes you feel weird, get out of the bed.
- Don't get frustrated with her for having period pain, just because you don't understand it. She doesn't owe you a hand-job that week. You can take a few days off from sex. Instead, get her a couple of Nurofen (don't forget water), a cup of tea and a hot water bottle. Leave her alone and tell her to text you if she needs anything. Imagine being kicked in the nuts repeatedly for a few hours, then give her the level of sympathy you would require until the pain stopped. But if her period turns her into a monster three weeks a month, it's OK to not want to stay in that relationship.
- Never laugh at her body, even if she laughs at yours. Stay strong, walk away, you can do so much better and she's not worth it.
- Never express disgust at the smell of her poo, and always crack a window and use a loo brush after yours.
- Never tell your friends what you did in bed unless you can trust them not to spread private details about her around school. Protect women from this at all times. If you hear a rumour about someone else, tell the person who told it to you that they are a massive dick and do your best to end it there.
- And finally (as I hand them both a condom) put this

> in your wallet and use it before your penis goes anywhere near her vagina. If you don't, you are likely to get a disease that will make your willy fall off, and you also might make a baby, that I am not looking after for you.

That's it, kids, GO HAVE FUN.
(I'm going to ruin them, aren't I?)

I wanted boys. I really think that my experience as a woman has given me what it takes to raise good men, and the challenge of it thrills me. We found out what sex Art was, but with Valentine it was a surprise. We only had a name for a boy, and I was hell-bent on it. I wanted to say 'Valentine' every day for the rest of my life, the thought of it made me so happy. For months we'd been trying to come up with a name if the baby was a girl. We went over and over so many, but nothing stuck. Over one dinner, I said I wanted 'a word'. Not a name, but a word. Like, Rebel, but not Rebel. And then I yelled RISKY across the room. We loved it, we were so happy. That was it, little Risky. As we got into the cab home, Chis said, 'That's a dog's name though, isn't it?' And I had to agree it was. Instead, I named a character Risky in my novel *So Lucky*, because I do still think it's a fun name.

When Val came out of me, at home on our bed, and I saw him underneath me (I was on all fours), I said, 'Valentine, it's you.' I knew it was going to be him. He was who I wanted to be in there. I was so happy I had my two guys. Just like my sister did, just like my best friend. Just like the aunty who raised me, and it all felt entirely as it should be. Art was in love with his brother from the start, and their friendship has been one of the most beautiful things I have ever witnessed blossoming. Especially in lockdown, knowing they have had each other was such a relief. They got on well before, but the bond they formed when they had to be there for each other to that degree, was nothing short of magical.

I think I wanted boys for a few reasons. 1) I understand men. 2) I want the next generation of men to be better. 3) I would worry less about them and 4) I love effeminate men and I wanted some of my own.

I love flamboyant men who wear pinks and florals and sit with their legs crossed (hello Chris O'Dowd). Men who don't say 'errr awkward', or 'what the hell do I know' when issues like menstruation, childbirth or boobs come up, make me tick. Men who can talk about women's bodies without immediately sexualising them because they don't know how else to talk about them are my HEROES. I LOVE good men. Tough guys with big hearts. Guys who love kittens. Friends' husbands who text you on your birthday rather than not bother just because his wife has done it. Guys who cook, who help with laundry. Men who hug men and kiss their friends on the cheek without then having to make 'I'm not gay' jokes. Men who do charity work. Men who attend the Women's March because they want to make their mothers proud. I LOVE men who make women laugh but don't get intimidated when women are funnier than them. I love men who are into sport but don't turn into rude robot morons when it's on. I love men with big appetites who ask you how you made something. I adore men who don't talk over women, who listen and ask questions. I can't get enough of men who don't see childcare as what a mother does. I love GOOD MEN.

There are so many brilliant men in this world and I am

excited to add more to the pile. I won't put the pressure on them to be perfect people, but I'll do my best to guide them in the right direction and hope they work it out.

There are a few things that have fascinated me in terms of typical 'boy' behaviour. Art's first true love was cars. He was obsessed, taking no less than twelve to bed. His face changed shape when he saw a toy car, like it was an ice cream covered in caramel sauce. Then there were planes, fire trucks, diggers, dinosaurs and all of the other 'typical' boy stuff. To be fair, it's not like I was waving Barbies under his nose, but he seemed genetically predisposed to like things with engines or wings. I do think that, no matter how we try to raise great men, boys will always be boys, and that's just fine. As long as they don't try to finger sleeping girls at parties then I'm here for it.

Here are the top things I've learned about raising boys in lockdown:

1. Don't watch them wrestle, it's too stressful.
2. Don't run out of peanut butter.
3. Don't try to answer their forty million questions about dinosaurs, because they are only asking you them so they can answer.
4. Watch where they put their feet.

PIECE SEVEN

Grief. It Hurts.

18 April
Isolation Update – She's in the air

I can't imagine there are many readers here who don't know about my friend, Caroline Flack, who took her own life in February. Caroline was, quite simply, one of my favourite people. She made me laugh more than anyone else could. Those agonising belly laughs where you cry your eyes out and wet yourself all at once. She was also fiercely loyal, and we really loved each other. Her death has made this entire experience extremely confusing. Is this isolation a blessing, or a curse? I have no idea. But Caroline has been throwing signs at me like fireballs and I've been catching them all and clinging onto them tight.

We woke up yesterday morning to total mayhem in our garden. Some undisclosed beastie had attacked anything inflatable or plastic that they could find; it was far too aggressive for the O'possum. It had torn the kids' goggles and water pistols, along with countless other hideous plastic crap that we have as a result of these animals that live in my house. It was hard to decipher what or who was responsible for this destruction, as not only were there about ten crows going bananas above our heads, there was also a raccoon on our deck acting like he owned the bloody place. He was so chill, sunbathing right above my head with no bother at all. He didn't seem like a plastic-ravishing kinda guy, so my guess was the crows. They dive-bombed us every time we walked outside (no, you screamed), and then I learned that crows have funerals. Apparently, when one dies, they throw an event. Which is fucked up, because as they continued to draw my eyes to the sky, a plane started writing the words 'Be Kind' and a huge love heart, right above my house.

I could not believe what I was seeing. Caroline's death had kicked off a social media campaign called #BeKind; then there they were, those words being written above my house, when I was already having a straight-up weepy moment about her and had had a particularly bad night. And then her sending the crows in so I didn't miss it. It's all a bit obvious, isn't it?

I feel her in everything. More than I have any other person I have lost. I feel like she is watching out for me in so many ways, and also just watching me, which I love. I miss her so much. The heart lingered in the sky for ages. I stared at it in disbelief but also let the power of the words in the sky seep into me. She did it, I am sure of it. I winked at the letters as they disappeared, and gave her a smile, wherever she was.

I stood under the big blue sky and took in a huge breath. She is in the air. She is everywhere. Whenever I need her, I can have her, if I just stop, and breathe in deeply enough.

I felt very calm for the rest of the day.

Last night, Art ran up the corridor yelling, 'Mummy, Valentine broke a pillow in the spare room.'

Oh God.

I followed him back to the spare room and there was Valentine, naked on the bed, smashing a cushion up and down. The final feathers shooting into the air, falling slowly into a large heap on the bed. He looked at me like he'd just won *Who Wants to Be a Millionaire*.

Luckily for me, Chris walked in and saw the look on my face before my rage exploded like the pillow. I could NOT be bothered to deal with it. He told me to clear off, and proudly went to get his little hand-held hoover. (Men love those, don't they?) I was grateful. Valentine ran after me asking if there were birds stuck in all his pillows.

I said yes.

I ate too much yesterday and really struggled at bedtime. Rather than bath our children, for the third night in a row, because we are brilliant, Chris and I sat on the deck drinking wine and eating crisps while the kids watched *Minions*. I was so full before I even got dinner out, but I still ate it all (TWO SAUSAGE ROLLS). By 11 p.m. I had to take my trousers off and I lay in bed like I was going into labour. I promised myself I would do a Peloton today to make up for it.

I did not do that.

I blocked someone on Instagram who got cross because I mentioned my grey hairs. I'd done an Instagram story about them, asking what I should do, and she sent me a message saying something along the lines of 'But you're not dying so get over it.'

I felt rage. Actual rage.

My biggest issue with social media is how people talk to those in the public eye, like if they're not mentioning something on their feed they're not thinking about it. Also, if they say something trivial, they are vacuous. I HATE IT. I am going grey and I am thinking about what to do about it. ALSO, a deadly pandemic is sweeping the globe and we are all stuck in our houses. BOTH can happen at the same time. Personally, I think this is the time to celebrate the intimate, mundane and trivial aspects of all our lives as a much-needed diversion from the 'YOU ARE ALL GOING TO DIE' media that is being shoved down our throats as soon as we sober up. Ya know?? I ALSO could have mentioned that I raised a few hundred for Choose Love today (I'm on an app called Cameo, where people pay me to make videos for them and the money goes to CL), like I do most days, because OBVIOUSLY I care about the world. But I'm going grey, you FUCKWIT, and that also deserves some airtime.

I blocked her and then swore, rather than swear at her then block her. As I have learned (ALTHOUGH IT IS HARD) that that is a better way to deal with these things.

I made a chicken curry. I worked hard at it while the kids were having some downtime. It was STRESSFUL because I didn't read the method first, and it needed a blender that I don't seem to have. Also, it was called a 'BAKED Chicken Curry', but I tried to be kooky and cooked it in a casserole on the hob instead of in the oven. I BURNT the bottom, and I am devastated. It's salvageable, but not ideal. GUTTED. I mean WHY couldn't I just do what it said?

But that is tonight . . . burnt chicken curry and *Jaws 4*, I can't wait. It's 5 p.m. and I just ate a weed cookie and had a margarita. We survived another day and life is OK. EVEN THOUGH I AM GOING GREY.

I love you all dearly (that's the drink talking). And I can't wait for dinner (that's the weed).

Love Dawn x

PS BE KIND.

21 April
Isolation Update – Please could you put your bum away at the table

On Saturday Art woke us up at 6 a.m. by asking Alexa to read him a story. She was set to a very loud volume, so I freaked and ran in shouting. He then had a meltdown because he couldn't work out how to get his dressing gown on. I didn't mean to be cruel, but it was quite funny watching him put his legs in the armholes, so I didn't help him for a while. I get my thrills in weird places these days.

When we came into the living room Lilu was howling at a billion decibels because she didn't have any water. It wasn't even 6.15 a.m., and already I felt like my head had done a few rounds in the tumble dryer. Then, at around 7 a.m., Valentine woke up. I thought he was coming over for a cuddle but he handed me a slug. I wondered what other delights the day had in store for me.

Did I tell you Valentine is one of those kids who, very possibly, sees the spirits? He does this weird thing, and it started two weeks after Caroline died, where whenever I ask him what a toy is called, he says 'Carrie'. It's so strange, because I haven't seen anyone called 'Carrie' in any of the shows he watches. I have a very close friend called Carrie who was over a while ago, but they haven't spent much time together. Also, I never called Caroline 'Carrie', so he didn't get it from me. But most people close to her did. So, I know it's a coincidence, and I know it's stupid, but WHERE THE HELL DID HE GET CARRIE FROM AND WHY DOES HE KEEP SAYING IT????

Kids are terrifying. One day, they're going to take over the world.

On Saturday I made us all AMAZING quesadillas, and at noon we sat out on the back porch with nice music playing, and ate them all up. In silence. The four of us. It was one of those rare and dreamy moments that I fantasise about. A glimpse into the future, maybe? Where we all sit and eat, and just relax. Rather than the food fights, me constantly yelling 'Eat your bloody food!' 'Stop throwing your food.' Or 'PUT YOUR ARSE AWAY AT THE TABLE.' It was nice. I enjoyed it. I needed it. Hope.

Since I last wrote, I have done two thirty-minute Peloton classes, but I still feel like my clothes are going to split at the seams. The eating is too much, I HAVE to stop. It's like every day is Christmas. My elaborate lunches, the crisps, the wine, the cheese board, the HUGE dinners. It brings me so much joy to make all this food, and I am so grateful we have it, but seriously. Truth is, I think it's what is keeping me together. The little missions I set myself every day while the kids have some downtime. I put on an audiobook, I pour wine, I find recipes, I make the food.

The problem is, then I eat it. All of it. Even when I make extra for the next day, Chris and I eat it all. But you know what? Fuck it. The Peloton keeps me a little bit fit, and I have no need for a bikini body when I can't even go on a beach. Also, it's blatantly the 'munchies', so the eating is here to stay because there is no way I'm dropping the weed. It has become my NUMBER ONE coping mechanism, even more so than booze.

In the afternoon, while Chris took Valentine for a walk to get him to sleep, Art and I made volcanoes out of egg cartons. I was so proud of myself. I didn't even Google it, I INVENTED it. I turned the egg carton upside down and cut around the cone shapes. We painted them different colours. Then I painted some red on yellow paper and cut it into strips – FIRE. I made a hole in the top of the cones, shoved in the flames and THEN WE HAD VOLCANOES. I know, I know, I'm just that kind of mum. All arty and craftsy. Just being me over here, move along.

The mosquitos are back. They're such a problem here in Los Angeles. MASSIVE ones, and Art and I are apparently their favourite snack. Chris and Val get bitten, but Art and I get munched. For years I've been using pathetic bug sprays that companies say are good for us, 'natural', because they don't have DEET in them. You know what's even better? Not getting eaten alive. Also, sitting in my garden is more important than avoiding harmful chemicals, so I am using the old school ones with DEET in again because the other ones do not work! I did some research, and it's not that bad unless you use tons of it or ingest it. Why would I ingest it? Does it have alcohol in it?

I need to take some milk thistle. I can hear my kidneys screaming.

Bill Gates said on TV the other night that he is backing vaccination research and they hope to have one by the end of NEXT YEAR. Just popping that here, so you can all throw up in your mouths.

Isn't this all so LOL?

Last night (Sunday) I made us all baby back ribs with potato salad, green salad, corn and a celery, apple and onion salad. We have a new pact, that we will eat as a family on Sundays.

It was awful.

The kids were being insane. Naked bums in the air, hyper, hysterical, not eating. I mean, the food was AMAZING (obvs), so why don't two-year-olds appreciate the concept of multiple side dishes? I got mad at the chaos, and even though I had tried not to all day, I ended up opening a bottle of wine. IT IS HARD.

Until tomorrow, my friends,

Love Dawn x

22 April
Isolation Update – I AM SMILING UNDER HERE

I had three glasses of barely drinkable wine last night, and today was bad.

I didn't want to wake up. Then Chris said Lilu had shat everywhere in the living room. Then Valentine went mad at me because I tried to put trousers on him. I could have ended the day right there, to be honest.

But of course, it went on, and on, and on.

Chris took the kids to the park, and I walked to the shop to get food. At the shop I got sad about everyone wearing masks. I miss faces. I'd forgotten my mask, so wrapped a fabric bag around my face. I felt stupid and conspicuous, then realised the effect wearing masks will have on our identities, as in, who cares if people thought I was weird for wearing a bag around my head, no one knew it was me, did they? Is that a good thing, or a bad thing? I just don't know. It didn't feel good today.

The woman on the cash register had just sprayed the counter with anti-bacterial spray and it was soaking wet. I was halfway through putting something on it when I realised, so I pulled it back towards me and stood waiting, presuming she was about to wipe it. She thought I was being rude. 'It needs a moment to sterilise,' she said. 'God, I'm just trying to stop people getting sick!'

I was mortified, I wasn't huffing at her. Quite the opposite, I was grateful for everything she was doing. The only reason she thought I was angry is because she couldn't see my smile. I hated that. How many terrible arguments will happen because people's smiles are hidden? Urgh. That expression 'you should have seen the look on their face' will become obsolete. It upsets me, and today it made me cross and sad. And that sadness escalated to full-throttle frustration and grief, and then I could barely stop crying all day.

Grief got me today. It wasn't great.

The kids and I made pizza for lunch, and after that I took them in the pool. I sat on the side as they screamed and shouted and kept talking and talking and moaning and complaining that I wasn't going in. I tried not to snap, to let their words merge into one loud easy-to-block-out noise, but I couldn't do it. I was getting annoyed, I wanted everyone to SHUT UP. Then Chris came out to say hi, and he hugged me, and that was when the floodgates really opened, and I went inside and I took a moment to fall apart, and after that things did feel better.

It was just a shit day. I haven't had many of them, and that makes me lucky. But when they come, they come hard, and there is nothing I can do about it.

I know I've touched on this before, but I do think we are all being taught a bigger lesson than we realise from all of this. For me, the emotional roller coaster I've been over the last two months must be teaching me something, right? One of my best friends takes her own life, then the world goes on shut-down the very next week after her funeral. Making me face grief in the most unusual way. I am forced to parent in a way that I have never had time to before, I am in contact with a small but loyal group of friends. I am speaking to my family more. I am working on my marriage more. I am nesting, organising, preparing for disaster, making sure that, if the world goes to shit, we will survive. I am loving harder than I've ever loved in my life. I was alone with my grief, but now the whole world is grieving too. A solidarity that we can't deny. The good, the bad, whatever our experience of this, we are all in some version of it together. All we can do is love. Maybe those of us who were drowning in sadness are lucky to have this group experience, to help us move on? I dunno.

It's nice. And it's odd for me to feel that anything is nice, because what happened to Caroline was the worst thing that's ever happened to me (not just me, of course. So many people are hurting. Caroline has so many good friends), but somehow, with all that's going on, I am being forced to find the positives and I think I'm getting a grip on what they might be. But I fucking miss her so much. She's on my mind every second of every day. On top of that, I'm worried about the world. It's a lot to think about, but a real lesson in keeping your feet on the ground and focusing on the things that matter . . . love. Love is all there is. And crisps. Love and crisps.

Someone needs to write that song.

Once I did a post on Twitter that said, 'Crisps save lives.' Caroline thought it was hilarious and messaged me about it. She then said it all the time. Even crisps remind me of her.

Hope you're all OK. Tell me tales from your homes.

Love Dawn x

PS Halfway through writing this, Chris called me outside. I went out to find him on a chair with Valentine asleep on him. Knowing I'm having a shit day, he stood up, gave me his chair, then put my sleeping baby on me. I sat there, Valentine slumped onto me like the delicious dollop that he is, and I breathed him in. It was the medicine I needed. Almost as good as wine. It's going to be OK.

When the World Stopped Turning

Nothing like lockdown to make you flit so dramatically between the gargantuan and trivial aspects of your life. After Caroline died, I'd find myself in floods of tears because I missed her so much, then immediately snapped out of it by a small child asking me for a rice cake. Kids are a useful distraction, I think. Although there were times when I longed to sit alone with my sadness, to have no one take me away from it and just sob and sob until it got easier. I guess the worry with that is that it doesn't get easier. Or that, in the time you take to wallow, so many other aspects of your life get ignored that when you get back to it, you have a huge mess to sort out. Maybe having two small people who give you little time to sit with sadness is a good thing, though there are days when it really didn't feel that way. I hid most of my grief from them. I never tried to explain to them that my friend had died. I felt that being kept home with no mates and me not being able to get their favourite brand of peanut butter was enough for them to cope with, rather than their mum being someone they had to be worried about. They are so young.

Grief is an all-consuming emotion that you cannot fight in

the early stage. People have always spoken to me like I know about it, because of my mum's death a few days before my seventh birthday, but honestly, until recent years I really had no idea how hard it was. We'd lost two very close family members a few years ago (on Chris's side). It isn't my place to talk about it here, but it was a very sad time. Both had been ill for a while, so there was a certain amount of mental preparation that could be done. I don't know how much that actually helps the people closest in those times, as the reality is the people they love still just disappear, but the total shock of Caroline's death was certainly a huge part of the pain.

I didn't see it coming. It's like a car bursting through your living room window and setting your house on fire while you were watching trash TV. A catastrophic shock where everything feels destroyed in a heartbeat.

It was 7.30 a.m. on a Saturday morning here in Los Angeles, just moments before the news broke publicly in the UK, when I got the call from Josie. Of course, my reaction was shock and disbelief. All the obvious feelings that people talk about after something like this happens. I cried immediately. The kind of tears I'm not sure I've ever cried before. It was guttural. I sobbed hard and out loud. No space for self-awareness, no control. I remember my body shaking and my heart beating like I'd just run a marathon. Pins and needles up my legs, a pain in my head. I'd slept so badly the night before, I'd been up all night with terrible period pain. It's always bad, but this was particularly bad. I'd taken too many painkillers so had to stop but I was still really sore, so I just had to writhe around and deal with it. To think what was happening with Caroline while I was doing that. Was I feeling her pain too? I've come to a point where I think everything is connected.

After the call, a whole new pain started. This one emotional. I kept thinking it would never stop. How could it, unless it wasn't true? I then called a few people who deserved to hear it from a friend first, rather than on Twitter. When I'd done that, everyone seemed to know within minutes. Twitter was flooded with it. It was so fast. People were calling me and texting me, and I wondered when she would be in touch to tell me it was a hoax. My body detached itself from my head and went and tried to live a normal life.

We had plans to be at a kids' birthday party that morning and we went. I can't believe we went. The friends were British, it felt like being around people that at least knew of her would feel better. It felt like it would have been harder to be home with the kids all day, having to entertain them, that if we took them to a party at least they would have been out. Chris could have gone, but I couldn't be alone, I needed to be with him. He was everything to me in those moments. I didn't want to be without him. I didn't really know what I was doing. I put on a green dress that I had worn with Caroline at Glastonbury one year. I cried at the party and people talked about what had happened, but they didn't know her and I couldn't do what I wanted to do, which was fall to my knees and beg for it to not be true. The media was alive with the news that she was dead and all I kept thinking was 'She's my funniest friend in the world. This can't be happening.' But it was. I had to leave because my dear friend Mel was doing a performance of the *Vagina Monologues* and it meant a lot to her that I was there. She didn't know about Caroline yet, and I didn't want her to look into the audience and think I hadn't come. So I went. I kept telling myself that friendship was everything, I had to show up for her. Caroline always showed up for me. I sat with Mel's husband and his mother, who were very supportive but kept talking to me and I couldn't make out what they were saying. Luckily, Mel was on first and after she'd done her monologue I ran out. Sitting in that auditorium felt impossible. I needed to get home, and I needed to meltdown. I had to be with Chris.

While I waited for my Uber I stood on the corner of Highland Avenue and Hollywood Boulevard, scrolling through her Instagram feed. I read the texts she'd sent me days before. I stared at the last message, willing a speech bubble to pop up underneath it, but it never ever did. I was sobbing again. Loudly. People were looking at me, I didn't care. The world wasn't real. Reality was in my phone, it was going to light up any minute, and say it wasn't true.

I'm not going to share the final weeks of Caroline's life. That is her story, not mine. But what happened to me following her death is something I feel I need to share. Grief tore me in half. For months there was no space in my head for anything else. Even writing this, I still feel like I have 20 per cent of my brain on the job. I don't even know what I'm talking about – does any of this even make sense? Since that morning, I've been scared to look at my phone when I wake up, in case more bad news comes. When it happened, I was scared to be outside because I did crazy things like walk across roads without looking both ways. I should never have driven with my kids in the car, I wasn't safe. I found being with them a huge comfort, but I didn't want them to feel my heartbreak. I was so anxious and sad. I was also afraid. I didn't have any faith that something else terrible wasn't about to happen.

My main fear was that I had to continue to live my life as I did before, just to protect other people. When you lose someone, you get a lot of love and support, but soon, and naturally, that begins to fade away. I remember a moment around three weeks after she'd gone, where people stopped asking about it. The texts slowed down. The support bubble popped. People got back to their lives. People spoke to me like I should be doing better. I wasn't. That's when the sinking feeling of 'oh, the world moves on, but I am stuck with this forever' kicks in. The unrelenting torture of grief, knowing that nothing can fix it, is a frightening path to look down. It's endless. Too exhausting to even try to start moving forward. You're fucked, everything is fucked, and there is nothing you can do about it because they've gone. You don't want to be that person who can't recover, but when you wake up in the morning and get out of bed, it's as if you look back and your body is still lying there. You can't re-inhabit it because too much has changed. That's not your body any more, and neither is this head. You have to walk around broken, either pretending to be OK, or not pretending to be OK. Both equally as horrific. I felt so far away from home, I wanted to go back but I couldn't. I needed to wait for funeral details, as I could only do the long haul once without the kids. The wait was awful.

I can look back on it, even though it was only five months ago from writing this, and I do see that things have got easier. The fog has lifted, I can cross a road like a normal person, I can have other thoughts, I can feel happy at times. But I can't see how the anxiety will ever go. I wake in the night, every night, and the first thing I see is Caroline. It's as if my sadness sits by my bed, staring at its watch, waiting for my eyes to open. I learned to pack the sadness away for the day. Enough to get through it, anyway. But it was always there, tap-tap-tapping on my mind. I think it always will be. No one who loses someone they love tells you it goes away. They say it gets easier, but it doesn't go away. It's actually comforting, in a way. You cling to the grief the way you would cling to the person if you had your time with them again.

Grief is like a helicopter that circles over your head (I have this thought as I look up to the sky, there is one circling my house right now, a common sight in Hollywood). The sound fades away sometimes, but you can always hear it. Other times it's so close that it's deafening, frightening, even. You know it could spiral out of control and come crashing down on top of you at any point. Some days, it's all so agonising that you kind of wish it would.

I tell myself the human race is designed to cope with death and that of course time is the greatest healer. I know that and I believe it. But Covid-19 slowed down time and I cannot for the life of me work out if that is a good thing or not. As the months went by, I'd find myself doing so much better. I'd get through hours, maybe sometimes an entire morning without feeling sad and actually focus on something else, giving it my full attention. When it hit me again, I'd be aware of what I'd just achieved and see it as progress. Maybe I'd walked the dog and chatted to my dad, not mentioning Caroline at all. Or perhaps I'd done some exercise and got into it enough that my mind didn't wander back to her. At the start, I thought I'd never again get through an hour without crying. The problem now is that I have learned to cope within the parameters of isolation, but as soon as I step outside it I am at a total loss. As things open up a little and I see friends, if they so much as mention Caroline I feel just as I did at the start. Like a cloud of smoke immediately fills my brain. Tears impossible to hold back. My voice stutters, stupid embarrassing hiccups come out of nowhere. It makes me anxious that, when life goes back to normal, I'll go through it all over again because it won't be normal. Caroline won't be in it. I worry I have so much to get through before I'll be able to accept it.

The pandemic has been such a weird time to be sad about losing someone who didn't die at the hand of coronavirus. The relentlessly terrible news took the personal experience out of death. It became about numbers and predictions, and each and every case instilled fear into us all. Who next . . . you? Me? Dad? Sister? I felt like it got in the way of what I wanted to be feeling. I resented it at first – why couldn't this huge thing go away so I could get back to just me and my thoughts? I hated the distraction, I wasn't ready for it. Four months after she died, it felt like it had happened so much longer ago because so much had happened in the world. Other days I'd wake up, I still do, and feel like it happened yesterday. It's dark to think about how many people have lost loved ones in 2020, but it provides no comfort or solidarity to know it wasn't just me and those of us who loved Caroline. To think how many people feel this sad at the same time is unbearable.

I miss her texts. Four hundred of them coming in, one after another. I miss her silly jokes, her infectious laugh. Karaoke was always so fun; but now as it makes me think of her I don't know if it will be fun again. I just want to cry. It will never be the same. I'd like to come back to the UK but I don't get how the streets of London exist without her tiny feet strutting down them. I don't know how the world keeps turning without her laugh making it spin. I know, of course I do, that people move on and grief makes us stronger, rounder, more emotionally mature or blah blah blah, whatever people say. But also, it just fucking sucks. It sucks so SO hard. I feel like sadness is now just a part of who I am. Right now, whenever happiness creeps in, so does a feeling of guilt that she isn't around to share it. There will be times and places when that guilt is unbearable. I find myself often saying that things remind me of her, but the truth is nothing reminds me of her because I never stop thinking about her. To be reminded would mean she would have to be out of my thoughts, for even a minute. And that has not been the case.

I know I'm not alone. I guess all we can do when we feel this way is to accept it that some days will be OK, and some days won't. It's as simple as that. Along with grief should be a gratefulness to be alive, because there is nothing like death to make you realise that. But as much as it's important to rebuild, sometimes it's OK to just feel really, really upset. I've learned trying to fight that is just a total waste of time.

PIECE EIGHT

The High Life

23 April
Isolation Update – How fat are his feet?

Well, last night was about as relaxing as a kick in the fanny. We put the *Cats* film on (it's so weird), and about half an hour in we had to turn it off because Valentine woke up screaming. I ran faster than I've ever run in my life into his room, where he groaned, 'Mummy, my foot hurts.' I looked at his foot. Two tiny red dots. I'm no David Attenborough, but I know a spider bite when I see one.

MY BABY!

I called Chris in and we turned the lights up and looked at it. Chris was straight on the iPad googling images of spider bites and yup, that's absolutely what it was. No swelling, no major redness, but he had woken up because it was sore, so our parenting whistles were tooting (NO idea what that was supposed to mean). I stripped the bed and searched for beasties while Valentine waved his foot in the air. He seemed fine. No fever, so issues, just two red dots. But still . . . MY BABY.

The problem with googling something like 'spider bite' is that you're faced with sheer horror. Luckily, Valentine's bite didn't look like a black widow one, but it was the 'brown recluse' I was worried about because I see them a lot in the garden. They are the gnarly cousin of the black widow; not as reclusive as they sound, they love a good chomp on a human foot. I see black widows a lot too, but I presumed we'd have known immediately if he was bitten by one of those. Anyway, Chris showed Valentine the pictures of spiders and Val pointed at the brown recluse and said, 'That one. That one was on the grass and it bit my foot.'

Super.

I text a friend whose kid got bitten by one last year, and she asked if there was any swelling. I said no, and sent her a picture of Valentine's foot. She went quiet on text, and I immediately knew why.

'It's OK – that's not swelling, he's just porky,' I texted hastily.

'THANK FUCK, I WAS FUCKING PANICKING,' she replied.

My sweet baby and his big fat feet.

We did some more searching and saw that most spider bites are nothing more than a bee sting, but we obviously didn't trust that. I put Valentine in my bed, so he could sleep with me. The plan being, if he seemed in any discomfort at all, I would take him straight to A & E. I also left a message for the doctor on call at his paediatrician, who called me back quickly to say that really, the only spider bites they worry about in LA are the black widows, and if he had been bitten by one of them, I wouldn't be calling her, I'd have gone to the emergency room hours ago. Cripes.

But still, I wouldn't let him out of my sight. It was a horrible hour, mostly because the last place we want to go right now is a hospital. Of course, I would have gone, but the idea of adding to what those amazing staff at hospitals are dealing with, or putting Valentine in danger of getting coronavirus and, urgh, no thanks. I am glad I waited for the doc's return call, because for a second there I was just going to go.

Luckily, all that ended up happening was Valentine and I had a lovely sleepover, and I was awoken gently at 7 a.m. by him stroking my face. It was 100 per cent gorgeous.

It made me think about all the danger that lurks here in California. People go on about Australia being bad, but we have some rotters here too. Black widows, rattlesnakes, mountain lions, coyotes, all sorts. Most of them will never bother us, but it does happen. A friend of mine was bitten by a rattlesnake last year and it was AWFUL. Like, AWFUL. He just made it to hospital before his limbs went numb, I mean JESUS. We take the kids to Ojai a lot (a gorgeous little town a couple of miles out of LA, feels like Italy, apart from the rattlesnakes, bears and mountain lions) and we roam the countryside. I love seeing them frolic, but I am so aware that when they run into long grass there is a significant risk of rattlesnakes, so I do a lot of screaming. In the UK the worst thing that can happen is probably getting stung by a wasp, but here the snakes and spiders are legit. I wish I could be more relaxed about it, but with kids as young as mine, it's quite scary to think what could happen. But hey, makes no sense to live in fear, so as I go to the supermarket to get food during a pandemic, my kids will continue to run freely outside. I do a lot less screaming in the supermarket.

I've had a MUCH better day. I think sometimes you just need to be sad, don't you? I got a lot out with my big ugly crying yesterday, and today the weight on my shoulders had lifted.

We had corned beef and mustard sandwiches for lunch, and all is well in the world.

Ooo, apparently there was quite a strong earthquake at around midnight last night, that woke loads of people up. Not me and Valentine though, which is weird. Isn't that exciting, and just what we need, a fucking earthquake? Hopefully it was just Mother Earth reminding us that today is her big day. READ THE ROOM, EARTH.

Happy Earth Day to you all. What a ride the human experience on this amazing planet is. Aren't we lucky to be a part of it?

Oh, stepping away from Mother Earth to her cruel digital sister, I hate Zoom conference calls. Work ones or friendly ones. I find them all awkward. Maybe I am just not doing enough, and I would get used to it if I got more involved. I do miss people. Maybe my next week resolution will be to do more socialising on my computer. Hmmm, maybe not.

Chris just handed me a gin and tonic. It's 4.10 p.m. Isn't he marvellous?

I didn't eat weed today and have eaten substantially less crap. The munchies are no joke. I'm not one for weighing myself, but I do try to keep my weight around 140lbs. I can get into all my favourite clothes if I am there. It is an achievable weight for me that means I can generally eat what I want if I do moderate amounts of exercise.

Guys, I accidentally weighed myself this morning and I was 148lbs. I was quite stunned. I had wondered why nothing fits. How did that happen? I guess after Caroline died, I just stopped working out and comfort ate. Then isolation started and since then I have done NOTHING but eat, and the small amount of exercise I do just isn't enough. I mean, it's fine, I have nowhere to go, but I don't like it when my favourite clothes don't fit me, because they make me happy. So, I am going to try to pull back a little. To start, I'll lose the crisps. Today I just had hummus and crackers as an afternoon snack, which tasted like feet in comparison to Kettle Chips, but I know it was a lot healthier.

That's about the only sacrifice I'm willing to make though; I need the wine and the gummies every now and again, and my big dinners bring me so much joy. I will also step up on the movement. Twenty minutes a day of exercise, even if it's just a dog walk. That's what I will aim for. When I start to see results, I'll roll the crisps back in. THAT, my friends, is a plan!

I'm cooking tacos tonight. Chris hates fish, so spicy fish tacos is my best bet for getting him to eat any. I really go for it with my sides. Let me talk you through it, because if you've never made tacos, it's a really fun dinner to have once a week. This is how I do it.

Buy a sachet of taco seasoning, either mild or spicy, depending on what you like. Fry either beef mince, chopped chicken thigh, vegetables or fish (I use tilapia), and add the seasoning. Have a reasonable amount of oil it in, it tastes yum.

Serve with small, soft and round corn or flour tortillas

Do any of these sides . . .

Cherry tomatoes, chopped small with spring onion, salt and pepper and lime juice. (I use a real lime for this and save the sacred lime juice in the bottle for my drinks)
Grated cheese
Black beans (warmed up)
Hot salsa
Mild salsa (verde)
Chopped cabbage
Chopped onion
Sour cream
Guacamole (or just simple smashed avocado)
Sweetcorn
Hot sauce

Those are my regular toppings, I do them all in little bowls and we make taco after taco as we watch TV. HEAVEN. Try it, you WILL deffo get laid if you make this for a lover.

SENDING LOVE,

Dawn x

PS I have a wine delivery coming in a minute and I am SO excited.

24 April
Isolation Update – I wasn't quite sure how I would get across the room

As I was bathing the kids tonight, I lifted my dress to look at my body in the mirror. A nasty thing to do to myself, since I'd taken on the task of eating nineteen meals a day since isolation began, but there we are. As I gawped disapprovingly at my belly, Art said, 'Mummy, are you pregnant?'

You know what? It's your fault I can't get a six-pack and my boobs swing around my back. Brush your teeth and bog off!

Who asked him anyway?

I think I told you that yesterday I didn't have a weed gummy. This was purely to avoid the munchies. I ate constantly anyway, but it was absolutely less than when under the mild influence of weed. But after dinner, when the kids were down, I felt a bit tetchy so thought I'd try one of my Indica gummies. I think it's important at this stage to admit that I know lockdown has turned me into someone who drinks too much with a daily need for marijuana edibles. This is what happens when you suddenly find yourself a full-time stay-at-home mum suffering from crippling grief, while a deadly virus lurks on everything from the pavements to the vegetables in the local supermarket. I need to do what I need to do to cope with the stress of it all. It's as simple as that.

If you don't know much about marijuana, there are basically two types: CBD and THC. CBD is lovely, but it doesn't make you high. It works only on your body, so it's great for pain and anxiety and sleep. I take it a lot, and it's relaxing. Kinda like an Epsom salt bath feeling with, like I said, no effect at all on your head. It's available in the UK and Ireland so you may have tried it. It's not really a drug, and it's finally being treated that way and being enjoyed for its many benefits. It eases PMT and is great for older people who ache (and moan). I may have sent some to my dad. HI, DADDY, LOVE YOU.

Then there is THC, and this is what gets you spangled. There are two types, Sativa and Indica. Sativa is what I usually take. It gets you high, lifts you up, and totally distracts you from your children. The gummies are strong, so I have a tiny nibble. I'm never looking to be off my head when I'm around my kids, all I'm aiming for is for a slight buzz to numb the agony of having to look after them.

Indica is different, it goes to your mind, but it really works on your body. People take it to chill them out. It's not a party drug really, as it makes you quite lethargic. I've not really taken it . . . until last night.

You see, when Caroline died, I went to Med Men, the Apple Store of weed shops. Most of the staff are millennials with the occasional older dude who has probably been smoking weed since he was six and thinks prissy girls like me who spend $30 on some candy are a betrayal to his drug. They all wear matching Med Men Ts and have technology attached to them so they can process your order anywhere in the shop. You show your ID to get in, they scan it, and then you're basically in Willy Wonka's sugar palace and everything tastes like heaven and will leave you high as a kite. I feel like such a dork every time I go, and often drop some consonants and speak in my most lackadaisical voice to seem like less of a mum of two and more of a bro. They see right through me, of course. It will never seem right to be sold weed by someone who is calling you 'madam'. Anyway, I wanted whatever would make it remotely easier to calm down, sleep, stop hurting so much, and get through a hard time. I was recommended Indica. But I never took it, because actually I discovered that trying to cope while feeling normal was the best option. But time has now passed, and I've changed my mind.

Last night, after dinner, I ate half an Indica gummy. Halfway through dinner my arms, legs and head turned into lead and I wasn't entirely sure how I was going to get across the room again. It wasn't scary, but I wasn't expecting it to be so strong. I went to bed because, as Chris said, 'Don't waste it' and I lay down and was asleep within minutes. I didn't wake up at all until 6.15 a.m., which is very unusual for me. It was nice. I didn't like how incapable I was when I was awake, mainly because I quite like being able to use my own arms, but that sleep . . . my goodness. I'll only have a tiny bit if I take it again, hopefully finding the perfect amount to be able to walk, but also sleep that deeply. I've felt amazing all day. Weed became legal here to help people with conditions like anxiety and stress. Well, that is what you suffer from when you lose a friend the way I just did, so I think I am maybe the perfect candidate for it right now. This isn't a version of weed I would usually take, it's too strong for me. But my God, that sleep. Even so, this is NOT an advert for weed, kids. It's strong stuff, don't fuck about with it.

All day I kept thinking WHY isn't it Friday yet, and then I'd realise it wouldn't make any difference even if it was.

I did a Peloton (because my kid fat-shamed me) and I didn't eat crisps or start drinking until five. Did I win today?

I bribed the kids with gummies (NOT marijuana ones) at 8.30 a.m. so they would let me put sunscreen on them, and it worked a treat. I'd ordered some new swimsuits for them which arrived today. They are full-body zip-up rash guards and they have totally saved the day. I got them blue and pink ones, and they loved them and wore them all day. So hopefully that is that problem solved. I only need to get the sunscreen on their cheeks now. Which, annoyingly, is the bit they hate the most.

Jesus, did I just write an entire paragraph about putting sunscreen on my kids? Is that the kind of content you're here for? RIVETING STUFF. Let's blame the weed, I'm still dreaming of that sleep.

Wouldn't it be fun if the government just admitted there was nothing we could do about Covid, and gave everyone in the world free weed gummies so we could basically be at Glastonbury for all eternity?

I should be president. Everything would be so much easier.

Sending you all my love,

Dawn x

Flying High in Lockdown

I've always had a good relationship with drugs. 'Good' meaning they always did what they were supposed to do. If I took them to party, I had fun. If I took them to sleep, I slept. All very straightforward. My twenties were about the party drugs. Raised on Guernsey, I didn't really have access to much until I went to drama school in Liverpool. Excuse my vagueness in the descriptions of what I got up to, but of course none of what I am admitting to is legal. So, for the sake of anyone official reading this, or my parents, or anyone who finds this awful, I'm totally making this up to sound cool.

Anyway, point being, I was lucky that I could always dip in and out of that kind of thing and gave it all up well before I had kids. It stopped being fun after a while. And I'm not really interested in recreational activities that aren't fun.

Remember how weird that first week of lockdown felt? It was like the apocalypse was coming and America was a terrible place to be. Anxiety was high. When I landed in LAX after Caroline's funeral, friends with government intel were warning me of imminent disaster. The National Guard was on its way to man the streets outside our houses, ready to wave their guns at us if we dared leave our homes. Food parcels would be thrown over our gates. Riots would erupt in the streets; violence would overcome us.

I found all of this very worrying, of course, but my most immediate source of anxiety was that the schools were starting to close. How would the kids cope with not being allowed out? No friends, no playdates? Art suddenly sitting at a computer every day instead of running around the schoolyard. It was awful, I didn't understand how anyone would cope. I had just been through a traumatic ordeal with Caroline passing away, I could barely think straight. The idea of not having at least six hours a day Monday to Friday to try to rebuild myself was, quite honestly, terrifying to me. I didn't want to be that sad around my kids.

Weed became legal for recreational use in California in 2016. Almost immediately, an overground industry was in action. It was slick, accessible and expensive. Weed stores popped up like coffee shops all over town. At first you needed a medical card to get in (administered by a doctor if you asked for one for emotional reasons. Easy to get. No real emotional reasons needed) but now, as long as you're over twenty-one and have a valid ID, you can get whatever you want.

I was never one for smoking spliffs. That thick, stinking skunk that the (mostly) boys passed around at college never did it for me. It made me cough, which was embarrassing, then pass out on the spot (also embarrassing). I thought it made people smell like dog beds, and no matter how much fun someone was having when smoking it, they were no fun to be around if you hadn't smoked it too. I hated what it did to people. The exact opposite reaction of what I wanted from drugs. When people referred to it as getting 'high', I never understood. When I smoked it, I felt like I was locked in a cupboard with all the lights turned off.

During my first year at uni I had a boyfriend who lived in a house with a bunch of lads. They smoked so much weed. A couple of them all day long, they just sat on the sofa and smoked and smoked. Always with a vacant, sleepy smile on their face, if they could manage one at all. They'd eat and eat then fall into hysterical fits of laughter about not much at all. They watched hours of daytime TV and occasionally picked up a guitar and played incredible music. They were smart and creative. The humour was high, but still I found it boring. As soon as someone lit a spliff, I remember feeling disappointed that that would be the direction of yet another day or night. The windows were never open; one guy barely left the house at all. Luckily for me, my boyfriend loved a smoke but wasn't as into it as the others, and he didn't seem to get as slobbed out by it. I like to think this was because of my fantastic rack, and how devastatingly sexy I was. (It wasn't. But hey, why not add some pizzazz to my memories.)

So, when weed became legalised here, I wasn't that excited about it. Living one house in from the grungy end of Melrose Avenue and alongside an alley with a certain kind of (human) wildlife inhabiting it, the smell of spliffs often made its way into our garden. I didn't like it. I didn't want it to be everywhere. I didn't want stoned peopled to be everywhere either. I found them annoying.

Quickly, vapes became the vessel of choice, and this was better and something I happily got involved with. I had some fun times walking around a bit buzzed at two in the afternoon (back in the day when we were allowed out). It's an easy way to get a little bit high. It was so much more fun than the low I remembered from skunk spliffs in the nineties (I don't know how to write about those without sounding like your gran). But I couldn't get past the coughing. It would always be the same. I'd casually accept the vape from whoever passed it to me (OH MY GOD, CASUALLY SHARING VAPES AT PARTIES, CAN YOU EVEN IMAGINE THAT AFTER COVID? WERE WE MAD??) then proceed to cough my guts up as we all pretended it wasn't happening and continued to try to have a conversation. Everyone else ignoring it too. I'd keep talking, through the coughing. Not wanting anyone to think I wasn't cool enough to handle it. I'm forty-one. This isn't OK. Smoking is not the one for me.

It used to be though – cigarettes, I mean, not weed. I used to love smoking. It all began when I was around ten and I stole some really important cigars from my uncle. No no, that wasn't a typo.

In the house I grew up in, behind the sofa on the window shelf was a small wooden box. Inside it were ten cigars. I used to open the box and look at them lovingly, I thought they looked delicious. My uncle was a pipe smoker. Every day after lunch and dinner, he'd sit and smoke a pipe. This is back in the day when smoking inside was perfectly normal. I loved the smell; he used nice tobacco in a yellow tin that he got from the tobacco shop in town. I used to buy it for him with a new pipe most Christmases, which can't have been legal, but hey ho, it was Guernsey in the early nineties and people didn't seem to worry about all that back then. I loved the smell of his pipe, so when I saw those cigars my hungry ten-year-old brain assumed it would be similar. Watching *EastEnders* also made me think that smoking was really cool. So, I took a cigar and, when my friend Diana came over, I made her come up the garden with me to smoke it. That's right, two ten-year-old girls hiding in a bush smoking a cigar, nothing to see here.

Then, over the course of a few weeks, I went on to smoke all of the cigars. I remember looking at the last one in the box and thinking, 'Oh God, what did I do?' but feeling what was the point in leaving just one? No one smoked cigars in our house, so maybe no one would ever know? And besides, I really liked them. So I smoked them alone along the cliff path when I was pretending to walk the dog.

I missed smoking after that but was far too young to buy any so needed to work out how to get my next fix. This is when I went into my uncle's closet and found a box of extremely fancy cigarettes. These were his travel smokes, as you weren't allowed to travel with pipes, apparently. So when he went away, he'd take these fancy fags, and have one of those instead. Until I smoked them all, that is. I smoked them out of my window, in the garden, at the beach and no one had any idea. It was brilliant, I was like a smoking ninja. Only one night, I messed up. I messed up real, real bad and, looking back, I still have no idea what I was thinking. One night, while my aunt and uncle were out and my cousin Loren was babysitting, I went into my uncle's closet, took the last cigarette and smoked it IN HIS BATHROOM.

Why, why did I do that? This was not a house with smokers in it. The occasional pipe, sure, but nothing more. And never upstairs. WHY did I do it? I have no idea. The smell must have drifted down the stairs to Loren's nose, because suddenly he was knocking on the bathroom door. I remember the feeling of fear. I'd been caught – why else would he be at the door?

I think I said something like 'Out in a minute' in a very high-pitched voice and he just stood there and waited. I had to come out. So I emerged, and he said, 'So you smoke, do you?'

I went to bed petrified and full of shame, and when my aunty and uncle got home they came into my room and told me off. I was in so much trouble. I remember while my uncle was telling me he'd have to start taking the bottles because I couldn't be trusted – he was right, I got into those a few years later – my aunty came up with the empty cigar box. That was when I discovered that a great friend of theirs who had recently DIED had left them the cigars. Their sentimental value was immeasurable. I'd smoked away their inheritance. At ten years of age. I am yet to live this down.

I went on to start buying my own cigarettes and smoking properly when I was about fifteen. A habit that I eventually gave up in my early twenties when my aunty became very ill and was in hospital. I sat with her for hours and days on end, occasionally going outside for a smoke. It struck me, one day, how ridiculous that was. There she was in ICU, the fact that she'd never been a smoker perhaps helping to keep her alive, and there I was, going for a fag. Suddenly smoking felt like the most stupid thing you could do. So I stopped, and that was that. I now hate smoking and give anyone I love a really hard time when I see them do it. I am a real asshole about it. So smoke next to me at your peril, you have been warned. After I quit, I hated smoking weed even more, so you can imagine my relief when I discovered edibles.

Of course, the idea of eating weed has been around forever and is nothing new. Weed cookies, brownies, pancakes, or whatever else anyone could be bothered to cook and sprinkle with the magic green herb. But California has come on a long way since that. Now we're talking about delicious gummy bears in pretty packets, decadent chocolates in fancy boxes, mints in elegant tins. The first time I ever had anything like this was after I was given a packet of some in a big Hollywood gifting suite. If you don't know what a gifting suite is, it is both amazing and hideous all at the same time. Around award season, brands want to get their stuff on celebrities, throwing free stuff at them. A gifting suite is either a back room at the event itself, or a place set up that exists for a few days before the event. People (mostly famous people) are invited to go and pick what they want. It's like shopping, but everything is free. Sounds amazing, doesn't it? And it can be. You can come out with some excellent swag. But it can also make you feel like a total dick.

When Chris and I were in our early days as a couple, we were at an event. Actually, it was my first ever red carpet and I was terrified and looked like shit. I think it was the GQ Awards. Someone came to get us from our table, and took us to the gifting suite. I was so excited. I went around trying things on and picking products. There were even those fish that gave you pedicures (GROSS), so I stuck my feet in and let them take a photo. Anyway, there was a top I liked. Everyone told me it looked nice, apart from the woman who was hoping Angelina Jolie had walked in, not me. Chris said, 'Can she have it?' AND THE WOMAN SAID NO. I had been invited into the gifting suite but I wasn't famous enough to have anything. It was SO awkward. My *Pretty Woman* moment. Chris, being amazing just said, 'Let's get the fuck out of here.' So we did. I felt gross all night. AND THEN, the picture of me with my feet getting munched by fish kept popping up everywhere, and I was like, I am not famous enough for your stupid top but you are happy to have me promote your manky toe-chewing fish?

URGH, I swore I'd never go to another one. But then we got invited to a big one in Hollywood and I told myself life was too short not to go. This was very different. It was so busy and had vibes of a commercial trade fair. A huge room with loads of different stalls where brands were displaying their best stuff. It was heaving with influencers that I'd never heard of but the cameras were going crazy for. We felt silly being there, but also, I wanted everything.

And now for the point of this story . . . one of the stalls was a marijuana brand. They had edibles and buds and ready-rolled spliffs, and I couldn't quite believe what I was seeing. They gave it to us for free. This was before weed was legal in California, so I had no idea how it was allowed and got my 'candies' home safely but with a certain trepidation. That afternoon, I ate one. There was very little information on the packet; in fact, there was none. No indication on how much to take. Nothing at all. An hour later, I was lying on my bed watching koala bears jump out of the hedge and into the pool. Also, Chris shaved his beard off and I didn't notice. I didn't move for six hours. Koala after koala. Luckily, this was before I was the mother of a child, because if the kids had been around, they would probably have turned into koalas too.

It was hard to know if I had enjoyed the experience or not. Being that off my head is only fun if it was the plan, which it was not. But I got through it and then threw the rest away. When weed became legal here, and gummies a popular way of consuming it, I tried again. Just a little nibble the next time, as there was still so little information on the packet. I enjoyed it a whole lot more. Being a bit high is really fun, being wasted to the point of seeing koalas is not what I am aiming for. ANY MORE.

Of course now vapes and edibles are commonplace in LA. It's as normal as seeing someone have a glass of wine, and when taken in the right amount, it's a much more pleasant drug than alcohol. It doesn't make you say mean things or feel like shit the next day. It helps with PMS and anxiety. It really is a mystery why it is illegal almost everywhere else. I think the world would be a much nicer place if everyone dropped alcohol and just had a mild marijuana mint instead. With the occasional margarita for those of us who can handle it.

My merchant of choice is a chain called 'Med Men'. Although I may have to go to a different location now because I had a meltdown last time I went. IT WASN'T MY FAULT. I drove all the way there to get these specific gummies that are quite mild. If I was to describe their strength, I'd say they are a bit like having a big glass of wine. I love them, everything is perfectly manageable having consumed one. ANYWAY, my driving licence was expired, but I didn't think that would matter because it still had my photo and date of birth on it. It did matter, guys, it mattered a lot. I told you about all their technology. Well, they don't just check your ID at the door, they scan it. When they scanned mine, it flashed red on the man's stupid machine.

'You can't come in,' he told me, LOVING IT. He was young and very cool, and he knew how cool he was because he was on the door of a fancy weed shop in Beverley Hills. To him, I imagine, it doesn't get cooler than that. (I annoyingly need to admit that he *was* quite cool.) ANYWAY, I said but look, I am married (flash my ring), I'm forty, and that is my ID – I'm just waiting for my new one to arrive.

He said no.

I asked him again. 'Oh come on, I'm in the system, I've been before.'

'No.'

'Please, I just drove here, the traffic was awful. I don't have time to come back.'

'No.'

And then I acted like an actual crazy person and really pissed him off.

'PLEASE,' I screeched a little too loudly. 'I HAVE TWO CHILDREN.'

He did not sympathise with my plight.

I haven't been back since.

Luckily, there is a delivery service. It's best I just stay home when I've run out of gummies.

My one complaint about the whole industry is the lack of information on what each piece of candy contains. The weed is measured in mgs, but who the hell knows what that means. If I eat this, will I be able to look after my kids, or will I lie on my bed for three hours watching koala bears jump out of the wall?

For me, the weed has been the perfect lockdown solution. I'm not sure if I would have needed it if I hadn't begun lockdown in the emotional turmoil that I was in, but I was, and I did. So that is that. It got me through it.

Beyond lockdown, however, this really isn't my party drug (these days that's tequila). It's just for me at home, possibly with a small group of good friends. I had a bad experience last year where I made a monumental tit of myself and since then have realised that if I want to be good in a crowd, marijuana is not the one. We were at a party and it was late. I'd eaten quite a strong gummy (5mg – too much for me) and I'd knocked back a few troughs of Whispering Angel (LETHAL). Chris and I popped outside for some air and got chatting with a friend. Moments later, two beautiful women approached us, one of whom, I got the impression, was quite well known. It turned out the two women were married and had two children together. We all shared stories of their cuteness and it was going very well, but then I decided to make a joke.

Art, my eldest, had red hair until he was three. It was amazing and I loved it and hoped it would stick around forever, but now it's more of a strawberry blonde. Anyway, sometimes I make jokes about it and on this night, I really FUCKING went for it.

'Yeah, I used to pretend he wasn't mine,' I lol'd. 'I rolled in that childcare until his hair sorted itself out,' I guffawed. I was unstoppable. I was being so funny, hilarious. Which meant it was weird that no one else was laughing. I could feel my friend's hard stare penetrating me, Chris's nails digging firmly into my arm. In the dim lights of the night air, a ginger hue started to glow on the gorgeous lady's head. She was the reddest of the red. Apparently a very famous redhead, actually. With very red-headed kids. When I realised, I panicked for a split second. But that didn't stop me. No no, not after those 5mgs of THC. I carried on, and on. I was, in no uncertain terms, being a total asshole, but I wasn't in control of it. It was like my mouth was one of those machines that spits out tennis balls, but instead of balls, all that flew out were insults. It didn't take long for them to make their excuses and say they needed to get home to relieve the babysitter, to which I yelled after them, 'I bet you do, you saucy minx!'

I know.

No, really, I know.

I woke up the next morning riven with shame. I couldn't understand how I'd managed to make such a mess of what could have been a perfectly pleasant encounter. I was so embarrassed. Horrified, in fact. Chris tried to make me feel better about it, but the words he couldn't bring himself to say were 'Oh it was fine.' It wasn't fine. I am an animal.

I felt I really needed to make things better, so I acquired her email address and wrote a heartfelt apology. I explained that I'm a mum of two who was tired and took a strong gummy, drank too much and that I am not usually so horrendous. I took full responsibility for being awful and told her not to be afraid to come to work. I would not throw more insulting vernacular at her. I expected an immediate response.

Days went by. Nothing.

Weeks. Not a peep.

At the time of writing this, NO RESPONSE.

So that was that. It was as bad as I had imagined. I did my best to make it right, but I guess sometimes you just push someone a little too far. There wasn't much more I could do. And then, a few weeks later I was dropping my kid off at school and there she was dropping hers. AT THE SAME SCHOOL. I mean, what the hell are the chances? On top of that, I noticed another child with her. The same age as Valentine. So they will almost certainly be in the same class when they start next year. Can someone please explain to me why the universe does this to good people? I SAID I WAS SORRY.

Anyway, the lesson here is; don't take anything that turns you into a lunatic and never make jokes about redheads even if your son is one and you think you have a ticket to do so. You don't.

I'm wondering if maybe home-schooling Valentine isn't such a bad idea after all?

PIECE NINE

Meanwhile, in the Animal World

28 April

Isolation Update – Rack off, bum clap!

Art came into the kitchen and I thought he was applauding me for making such excellent quesadillas but actually, he was farting. How can such a small bottom make such a large clapping noise? It really floored me.

I took Lilu and Potato to the vet today. They both needed shots. I took Valentine in the car, hoping that he would sleep. When we got to the vet, I had to park outside, call the vet, and wait for them to come and pick up my pets. I then had to sit and wait for them to be delivered back to me. Luckily Valentine slept, but the whole thing made me feel so sad. Then Val woke up and screamed blue murder for the next twenty minutes that Lilu and Potato were inside. He didn't even want the emergency raisins I had taken with me, and I couldn't get him out because the sun was so hot. So that was a massive fucking barrel of laughs – being stuck in a car with a screaming toddler for half an hour. What a total and heavenly joy.

The vet said Lilu has lost weight. She has, I can see it. She's so old. I've had her my entire adult life, I can't imagine being without her. Even if she did shit in the middle of the dining room today. Poor Lilu. The maddest person I have ever met, but my God, I love her. Did I tell you I'm going to get her stuffed when she dies? Yup. She'll sit by the fire forever and freak out every single person that sets foot in my house. But it feels like the right thing to do. She must exist for all eternity.

Bar the vet trip, I think I finally worked out how to relax this weekend. Without any writing to do, I sat on a chair outside whenever I got the chance and either chatted to my husband, ignored my kids, read a book, or listened to the radio. I feel like this NEVER happens, and it's largely my fault. I get four hours off the kids a day (Chris and I have a tight shift schedule that we are sticking to well) but always find myself working or cleaning or exercising (I'm just a fitness fanatic, guys, I can't help it). But I rarely do nothing, and you know what? IT WAS NICE. I must chill out more. Imagine getting to the end of isolation and feeling like you never sat down? What a total waste of government-enforced laziness that would be. Less pressure to perform, more pressure to perform world records in staring at walls.

I was thinking, there is a lot of pressure on artists right now. I feel it. My friends feel it. Like if we don't create something brilliant during this time then we have wasted an opportunity. I wake up almost every day with the feeling of 'OK, this is a great idea . . .' Then by the time I get the kids down I think to myself, 'You know what is a really good idea? THAT WINE.'

If isolation doesn't make us crazy, then the actual world will.

You may have heard Trump suggesting that they INJECT people with disinfectant to cure coronavirus? Such a good idea. Personally, I don't see what all the fuss is about. I'd also like to suggest fire and swallowing pins. OH, and licking the handrails on the Tube and sticking your finger up random people's bumholes. They might ALL kill Covid-19. TRY IT.

Don't. Don't try those things. I was joking. Apart from the random fingers up bums. People LOVE it, and you'll learn a lot about yourself too.

Do you know what is quite funny, though? In the kitchen a few weeks ago I was cleaning and I saw the 'KILLS 99.9 per cent of germs, can even kill the flu virus' on the label of the disinfectant and I thought, It's mad, isn't it . . . they know how to kill a virus, they just can't do it when it's inside someone. It must be so frustrating for scientists to know there is a thing that kills it, they just can't use it. AND THEN I thought, I better not ever say that out loud in case anyone thinks it's an actual idea and does it. AND THEN the President of the United States of America just SAID IT TO THE ENTIRE WORLD.

Come on now, if that wasn't the ammunition that the gun-waving Republicans need to stop pretending that giant satsuma cares about them, then what is??

OWN GUNS AND DRINK BLEACH.

Yes, Mr President.

On Saturday, Art picked Val up then dropped him on his head. It was awful. So, then we made cupcakes and they were MIND-BLOWING. Guys, I did it. I baked something and it was beyond perfect. Fluffy on the inside, crispy on the outside. I HAND-WHIPPED heavy cream until it was thick, then I coloured it pink and put sprinkles on top and oh boy! I was so proud. I'm now determined to come out of isolation unafraid of cakes.

When I was whisking the cream for the cupcakes I said to Art, 'This is really good exercise for Mummy's arms,' and he yelled, 'YEAH, MUMMY IS EXERCISING HER ARMS, FINALLY.'

SERIOUSLY, WHO ASKED YOU ANYWAY, BUM CLAP!

I have heat rash on my little toe and it's awful. I showed it to Chris and he got a bit cross that I had given him such a terrible visual. I won't show it to you, but please know it's dreadful and I deserve sympathy.[1]

Anyway, I'm making my first mushroom risotto tonight, never made one before. Isn't that exciting? I'm a little nervous it will be boring. I'm not sure how excited I am about a big bowl of rice for dinner, but I do love the idea of mushrooms, cream, butter and garlic so I'll give it a go and let you know how I get on tomorrow.

Love Dawn x

29 April
Isolation Update – Zoom fail

I'm sorry to tell you this, but my risotto was distinctly average. As I thought, just a big bowl of rice, no matter how many types of mushrooms I put in it. What a MASSIVE waste of wine.

Alas, wine is one of the sacrifices we must make when being experimental in the kitchen. But my God, it hurts when it doesn't go well.

I FELT SO LAZY TODAY. Morose, grumpy and uninspired. I screamed at my kids this morning and felt awful all day.

[1] Please do not forget this information, it becomes CRUCIAL in a few pages.

They were doing nothing wrong, really. Just being so loud and annoying, but nothing wrong. They just wouldn't listen to me, they kept arguing over toys. Then they kept ROOOARRRING and I just flipped. I won't tell you what I screamed, because it was unacceptable and made me sound like a lunatic; it was far from ideal. I then I went into the kitchen and had a bit of a sob because I felt like a horrible mum. Classic.

We made pizza for lunch and they loved it. It kept them quiet for thirteen minutes. And yes, I timed it. Are anyone else's kids living off pizza ingredients in various forms? Flour, cheese, tomato and salami? I'm either making that into pasta or sandwiches or pizza at least five times a week. LUCKY KIDS.

LA was supposed to be on 'Stay at Home' orders until 15 May. I'm happy to do social distancing for as long as it needs to happen, but I want to be able to have a small circle of people that we are allowed to see. I'd happily have my friends' kids here, anything to break the monotony. Then, of course, they could go there . . . for a week.

I realised that I need to go a little easier on myself, so I apologise if these entries are a bit shorter sometimes. Some days I just can't pull together. Also, when NOTHING HAPPENS it's hard to muster anything to say.

Anyway, tomorrow is another day.

Love Dawn x

1 May
Isolation Update – The Lady of the Flies

This morning was a blast. Art woke up drenched in wee and Lilu had puked, pissed AND shat behind the sofa. THEN, Art spilled a box of PINS into a huge box of stationery. It took me ages to get them all tidied up, and I stabbed myself no less than ten times as I did it. BUT I gave the kids wholemeal croissants (so LA) with jam and butter, and they were so grateful they were nice to me for ages after that. So, all in all, by 9 a.m. we were all on speaking terms, which was a great start to another day of this nonsense.

Now let's talk about something important.

Many of you who have followed me for a while may know that I am plagued by evil. Last year, I kept finding dead rats (their heads had exploded) in my garden, then I had mice, then a major cockroach infestation and now, my friends, I am at war with flies.

When the weather gets hot in LA, the flies come out in force. My kitchen – which is clean, before you judge me – is apparently their holiday home. I've tried all sorts. One idea was this ghastly bag of liquid that they get attracted to, go inside, drown and die. Oh my God, the smell. THE SMELL. No. So then I tried sticky traps, but I cannot deal with thousands of little dead bodies in my house. I've considered the big lights that zap them, but they are SO ugly. Also, WHY is there always some horrible creature trying to break me? I was having a lovely picnic with the boys earlier and we got dive-bombed by a mother fucking hornet. YOU CAN IMAGINE. I ran into the house then remembered I had children and ran back out. IT TRIED TO KILL ME.

I'm scared of so many things. Cockroaches, wasps, snakes, spiders, rats – the list goes on and on. I don't want to be afraid of anything, and when I am not in view of any of these things I talk to myself quite calmly. I say, if a cockroach was to run across the room now, I would be calm and logical. I would get up slowly, go to the kitchen, get a glass and a postcard, come back over to the bug, pop the glass on top of it, slide the postcard underneath it, and then walk calmly outside and put it on the street. I know I could be this person, if I tried.

But I'm not. What happens is quite different.

I see a cockroach and I run screaming to my husband: 'SAVE ME SAVE ME THERE IS A DINOSAUR IN THE KITCHEN.' I create drama and hysteria, I leave him no choice but to drop everything and rescue me, and he always does.

But seriously, what is it with the flies? I don't need a metaphor to remind me that we're living through a plague! Maybe I can train Potato to eat the flies. Or Valentine.

WHAT IS HAPPENING.

I can't cope with anything any more.

Oh, I want to talk about my nose. As you know, my nose is not normal. It has been likened to the Child Catcher from *Chitty Chitty Bang Bang*, and, less offensively, a ski slope. I have hated it for most of my life but have now grown to love it. I don't know where it came from, or why it is so weird, but it is my nose and it has served me well. Given the choice, which I have, I wouldn't change it. ANYWAY, I went to the shops to get food yesterday and wore one of my headscarves over my face like a bandana. In the old days, it would look like I was about to rob the shop, but now this is our normal. I took my time because it was so nice not being with my children and did my weekly enormous food haul. Back in the car, I removed my scarf and looked in the rear-view mirror. Guys, my nose was squashed. Like, totally squashed flat. An entirely different nose to my normal nose. I couldn't believe it. I had to circle it round and round for about a minute until it sprung back up into its natural pose. The nose pose I have grown to love and was so happy to see again.

Did I just write an entire paragraph about my nose getting squashed? I did, didn't I? RIVETING STUFF.

I better go.

Stay home, stay safe, and stay drunk.

In the meantime, I'm going to go fly-catching. SEND HELP.

Love Dawn x

PS Halfway through writing that I thought there was a cockroach on my arm and leapt a thousand feet into the air. It was actually a hair clip. Everyone needs to calm down.

5 May
Isolation Update – I'm a survivor

I have yelled the words 'Get to bed' around fifteen times in the past seven minutes. On the last one, I added a firm 'FUCKING' and, I have to say, it seems to have done the trick.

On Friday, Art and I got bored, so we painted Valentine green. I highly recommend this activity if you have a young child. Ideally, one that is young enough, and gullible enough, to believe that you can turn them into a frog. Val happily stood still for a good thirty minutes (that's a long time in parenting) while Art and I went at him with brushes and sponges (using non-toxic kids' paint, of course, don't report me), until Valentine was, indeed, a frog. He happily leapt around the garden making gross burping noises, while Art and I watched in hysterics, proud of our work. But then, after about six minutes, Valentine didn't like it any more, and I was instructed to 'GET IT OFF' because 'I WANT TO BE A LION' instead.

As you know, lions are not green. They are yellow. So then we had a problem. We'd just painted him green and we didn't have any yellow paint. A considerable meltdown expressed how Valentine felt about that, and the fun was very much over. I washed him in the pool, which turned green, and then put a nature programme about lions on the TV. I must say, this felt like a pretty victorious comeback. He was delighted.

On Friday night I ate so much pasta that I couldn't sleep. It's such a cruel consequence of consuming carbohydrates, isn't it? Agony. The feeling of maximum capacity. The unrelenting wind.

In other enormous news, I went for a Covid-19 antibody test and it was positive. *To the moves of Beyoncé* I'm a Survivor! I suspected I'd had it. Looking back, the symptoms started on the way back to LA from London after Caroline's funeral. I got a weird cough on the plane. I thought it was probably because I had done nothing but cry and talk for an entire week. But then a few days later, when Chris said Lilu had pissed all over the sofa and I couldn't smell it, I was suspicious. They had just announced that losing your sense of smell and taste was a symptom. But there were no tests, so I had no way of knowing. A number of my friends in London got pretty bad fever and flu-like symptoms the following week too. Mine were just very mild. If the media hadn't been yelling 'EVERYONE WILL DIE' in my ear, I would hardly even have noticed them.

Someone told me about a walk-in clinic in LA that had the tests. I called them, they sent a consent form, I paid, then I drove there. I waited outside and called again, a man came out with scrubs, a mask and a little trolley. (I must add that he looked at me in the car and asked ME if I was wearing scrubs, to which I said, 'No it's a floral tracksuit'. He judged me under his mask.) I wound down the window, he took a finger prick's worth of blood from my middle finger, then went back inside. Ten minutes later he came back and told me I had the best result he could give. I tested positive for IgG – long-term antibodies. Of course, no one knows what that means, whether I am immune and how long it lasts, but I got through Covid-19 unscathed, so it's good news either way.

It was so mad, sitting in the car waiting for the results. Firstly, it felt just like it did when I did my pregnancy tests: my belly was flipping, and I was desperate for it to be positive. I also had the radio on and found out I had survived this disease as they were announcing the latest death toll. It was so surreal and confusing and sad. How does it affect people so differently? It's so awful that it's a minor affliction for a portion of us but so deadly to vulnerable people. Which means we must all, and we must, take these unprecedented and extreme measures to stop it spreading. It's wild. Here I am, hardly even noticing any symptoms, but never wanting anyone to ever leave the house ever again in case my eighty-three-year-old aunty gets it, or my uncle, or my dad, or my in-laws, or any of my friends' parents, or anyone at all, for that matter. I may have immunity (do I? What's the latest news?), but I'll still wear my mask and take all the necessary measures, because I just have to.

But my GOD I hope the schools open again soon . . . I'm all for keeping everyone safe but FUCK ME I need some child-care.

I promised myself I wouldn't drink tonight, but here I am with a whopping great glass of red and Jamie Oliver's Chicken and Squash Cacciatore in the oven, a really tasty one-pot dish.

I annoyingly had the lid on the pan for the first half-hour of cooking so it might not be as gooey as it should be, but it smells incredible. Will serve with couscous and green salad. CANNOT WAIT. I must tell you though that NONE of my clothes fit. It's quite serious now. I found a jumpsuit that's basically egg-shaped. This will now be my uniform until I am not cooking like it's Christmas three times a day. Whatever.

I had the most massive craving for 1980s taramasalata today. The really sloppy, fluorescent pink kind that they sold in Bessant's, the supermarket on Guernsey back in the day. I remember the taste like it was yesterday. My mum used to get me a little pot of it (because it was more expensive than the cream cheese) and I'd eat it with a spoon on the floor, just like the classy bitch I have continued to be.

I keep turning to see Art cuddling Potato and it's really melting my heart. I love how pets teach kids to be sensitive. Cuteness.

I hope you had lovely weekends.

Love Dawn x

6 May
Isolation Update – My womb is stabbing me from the inside. So that's nice

Isn't being a woman awesome sometimes? The way you go to bed, think you're going to have a good night's sleep, but then your womb turns into a bag of knives that keep repeatedly stabbing you from the inside until you're forced to get up and lie on the living room floor, begging for the earth to open up and swallow you whole? Brilliant, isn't it?

I am forty-one and I have no idea what my body is doing. Two babies and an IUD mean my menstrual cycle is still trying to work out how to spin. It used to be two weeks of solid agony, a period, a week of feeling like I could rule the world, then back to a living hell again. That was the majority of my twenties, and a large part of my thirties, when I wasn't gestating. I have no idea what to expect and when to expect it, all I know is that for anything from two to eight nights a month, I will be in agony. Torture. But women live with pain, it's what we do, isn't it? We just get on with it. So in accordance with the deal we seem to have been dealt, without moaning, I get up in the night, take some painkillers, make tea, writhe in agony on the living room floor and then, when it starts to ease off, I go back to bed and barely even mention it the next morning. I mean, what the fuck? I cannot imagine a life where this doesn't happen, it's so normal. It's madness, utter madness. Why isn't someone in prison because of my monthly cramps? How is it not headline news?

Today was long. Every time I looked at the clock it was still the same time.

I did a Peloton this morning, so felt very smug until around 11 a.m. Chris had taken the kids to the park, so I walked around in workout clothes, pivoting up and down the hallway with a bottle of water. I put Lizzo on and cooked some eggs. Then I felt so tired that I sat on the sofa and allowed my eyes to slowly close. That is, of course, when the thunderous sound of my children coming home filled the house. I was then forced into a world of dinosaur make-believe, where I was asked well over 17 million times what my third favourite carnivore is. It took everything I had not to scream 'MY WOMB IS EXPLODING.' But instead I said what I always say when I am asked anything about prehistoric giant lizards: 'The T-Rex.'

They are always so pleased with my answer.

Chris tested negative for the antibodies, which has blown our minds. It turns out you can have sex with someone and not give them coronavirus, but you can't go to the beach in case it's on the sand. It is so confusing. How did I not give him this highly contagious disease?? Same with another friend of mine. She tested positive as having active corona, but her kids and husband didn't. How?? I'll never understand all this, the world has literally gone mad. No one knows anything. Do any of you know anything? Can you tell us anything? About ANYTHING? Honestly, anything at all?

Like I said, today was long. I've really lost steam and I need to get my energy back. I feel bad for Art. Some days he just hangs out and plays and wants stories and TV. And it's nice, but he is so unstimulated. At the start of all this I really tried (remember when I painted those pots?) but now I'm treating every day like it's Sunday and being so lazy. I must step it up. I need to get back to coming up with activities (like my volcanoes, remember those? Genius!) and I need to do better by him. I've been spending too much time looking at my phone and telling him I'll be there 'in a minute'. It's not fair. So please, WHAT can I do with him? He loves the baking, but we can't bake every day. He's a bit bored of painting and gets cross when I try to do anything educational. I asked him to say the alphabet the other day and he'd forgotten it, and I felt awful. He used to be obsessed with writing words but now gets cross when I suggest it. I've totally fucked it, haven't I? I did think of a fun way to do it though. If I go around the house and gather loads of his little toys, put them in a box, then he picks out five, one at a time, and writes the name of the animal down. That could work, and at least he will be doing something that involves his mind. God, it's so hard. He's five. He needs more. At this rate he'll go back to school and when they ask what he did in lockdown all he will say is, 'My mum ate ALL the pies.'

The garden is pretty at this time of year, but we keep getting attacked by a MASSIVE black bee. It's June-bug-sized, but shaped like a bee. Jet black and fucking loud. And I'm sorry to say that earlier this evening I learned something about myself that I wish I didn't know – when threatened by a big black bee, I abandon my children[1]. Here's what went down:

We were sitting outside. The bee flew close. I ran inside and later realised my baby was outside. Not ideal.

IN MY DEFENCE, Chris was outside. ALSO, I have a legit fear of everything. But no, I shouldn't have thrown the child at the bee, and then run inside. What I did was never going to save me.

OK, that's it from me tonight. Chris is doing a Zoom poker night with his mates, so I'm on the sofa with Lilu and Art is in my bed. I felt bad that I've been so boring, so suggested a sleepover to mix things up a bit. There are about 748 giant

[1] I did it AGAIN. Remember when I left my kids outside with the hornet? MUST DO BETTER.

fluffy cats on my side, so I'll snuggle up into those and hopefully Art won't wet the bed. My womb is firing up, I can feel it. Just as I start to get tired. Such is the curse.

You're all awesome. How were your days? Tell me anything.

Love Dawn x

7 May
Isolation Update – Munching on a rosemary stalk, like that's normal

Happy Hump Day! (Well it was at the time of writing.) I much prefer Hump Day to Slump Day, which was yesterday. Or Frump day, which is tomorrow. I'll make an exception for Pump Day, which is quite fun. But then of course there is Trump Day, which is every day. And that's a bag of bollocks.

ANYWAY.

My hair has been a disaster for so long that I can't imagine it not being a disaster. I was at the very end of what is acceptable before the pandemic hit, but I never made it to my hairdresser. So here we are, seven years later, and what is happening on my head needs to be stopped. Which, as it happens, might be possible because . . . until today I'd forgotten about my silk sleep hat. Long ago, before our leaders failed us and I left the house every day to go to an office, most days my hair looked quite nice. I had learned that if you sleep with a silk turban on, it protects your hair from your pillow. Which, you may not realise, is quite violent.

Most pillowcases are made of cotton. And cotton and hair DO NOT get on. Your hair sticks to it, so the friction mounts and by the time you wake up, all hell has let loose. But silk is much more silky (shocker, right?). Your hair is protected from your aggressive bedclothes, and when you wake up, it looks nice. I got really into the power of the silk turban for a while there, but since lockdown I've totally forgotten about it. Thus, I have been in constant combat with my nasty cotton pillowcase.

Well not any more. I wore the hat last night and actually quite liked my hair today. I mean, it still looked like shit. But better shit.

Earlier on I sent both the kids outside with a pair of (kids') scissors and told them to cut the grass. Didn't see them for forty minutes. HIGHLY recommend it. They did chop the tops off some of my favourite flowers, and some of the huge leaves off a tree, which wasn't ideal, but I got a chance to eat an entire packet of crisps without having to share them so, you know what, Mumma came out on top and that is OK too.

Do you ever imagine David Attenborough's voice commentating on you?

'The mother of this species is known for hiding her food from her young. She sends them out on dangerous and impossible missions so she can bury her face in her pantry and eat all of the carbohydrates without them seeing. She also attacks people if they go near her wine. And wears bright-coloured kaftans when she's in the mood for sex.'

Oh David, you know me so well.

IS IT STILL MAY?

The mayor of Los Angeles just came on the radio. He's saying a few businesses can reopen – kerbside pickup only. And that nature trails and golf courses are good to go. This is nice news. Nothing will be the same again, not for a long time, maybe never. But kerbside pickup is one step closer to me getting some childcare, so I am THRILLED.

GOLF COURSES THO? Isn't everyone who plays golf over seventy? Cos he then said no one over seventy is allowed to go out? This might be a good time to get into golf.

It is so weird listening to these announcements every day. So dramatic. Like watching old movies where everyone in a village shared a TV, and the clip in the film is of three hundred of them in one living room, glaring at a president on a 13-inch screen.

My munchies are out of control. I am cooking steak and roast potatoes tonight, but I have eaten half of Los Angeles already. I'm insatiable. A few minutes ago (I paused writing this to put the kids to bed), I found myself wandering around eating a stalk of raw rosemary. I mean, what the hell?

That's it from me folks. Until tomorrow.

Love Dawn x

8 May
Isolation Update – It's FaceTime, not BBC1!

Life with my cat is like having a mad, angry old lady who lives next door but somehow got a key to your house and comes round every day to scream at you.

It was Chris's morning with the kids, and I should have had a lie-in but Lilu had other ideas. Not only, according to Chris, had she pissed, shat and puked all over the living room (again), she wanted to tell me all about it. So, at 6.50 a.m., she screamed at my head at 384,791,823,918 decibels until I got up and gave her every shred of my attention.

Siamese cats are worse than babies. They scream like banshees. They go mad with old age. Get one at your peril.

Chris took the kids to the park and I did a Peloton. I felt *Lizzo voice* – SMUG AS HELL. I also finished a podcast I was doing and spoke to my dad because it's his birthday. So many things achieved by 11 a.m. The air was hot – this heatwave is intense. I felt like a zip-lock bag full of warm oil, so I sat on the couch and took a few moments to close my eyes and pretend I was in the Maldives with my best friend, Lou. It was at exactly that moment that the peace was shattered by the barrage of my family returning home. HOW DO THEY KNOW? Unable to cope with the onslaught of parenting, I put on the TV for them.

Hot weather is HARD. I mean, it's great when you're lying on a beach, or anywhere with a breeze and nothing to do, but in a garden with two small kids who WILL NOT shut up about dinosaurs, and refuse to wear sunscreen, and yell at you if you don't give them 99.99 per cent of your attention at all times, it's hard. I felt guilty about the TV, so turned it off. They didn't like that, so I gave them frozen lollipops, which got me a heavenly seven minutes of quiet. I sat and relaxed, willing the lollies to never end. Then Valentine dropped his on the floor and lost his mind. I wish I'd never bothered.

Because of the heat, we needed to be inside. I brought the big bag of Lego in from outside and tipped it all over the floor. From within the Lego emerged a small but deadly looking spider. I told the kids to GET OUT then trod on it with my foot, which only had a sock on it. Wasn't that brave? Remember when I ran inside and left the baby on the deck with the giant killer bee? I think we can all agree this is progress.

Poor Art has started to take after me. His reaction to the spider was dramatic. Valentine, on the other hand, ran towards it to pick it up. I swear one day he's going to put a black widow on me in my sleep. He has absolutely no fear. My job as a mother is to pass my fear and anxiety on to him. To protect him, but mostly to protect myself.

As I said, it was my dad's birthday. I sent him two sides of a really indulgent smoked salmon that he loves; he was very happy. My sister and I did our first group video call with him, and it was nice[1]. But obviously it took him twenty minutes to work out how to turn his video on, then we spent most

[1] It pains me to say this was the only time we chatted, all three of us together, in five months. MUST DO BETTER.

of it chatting to the upper right corner of his forehead. But still, it was lovely. We have such a small family on my dad's side. It's just me, Jane and him. A few years ago, for his seventieth, Jane and I surprised him. It took a lot of planning, Art was really little and I lived in LA, so travelling to Loch Lomond for three days was no joke. But we pulled it off. A day before his party, he was sitting in his local hotel with some friends waiting for dinner. When it was ready, Jane and I walked in with the food. I have never seen my dad lost for words – it was total magic. He'd been saying how sad he was that we couldn't be there for weeks, so I'm glad that we did it. Otherwise he'd still be sad about it. Sometimes making an effort like that can feel too stressful to bother, but we bothered, and it's a memory we will all have for life. I'm so grateful for it now. Who could have guessed that there would be a period of time in which we weren't allowed to travel? It's crazy. I am so glad for every air mile I ever flew to get to someone I love. I also keep thinking that if Caroline's funeral had been one week later, I wouldn't have been able to go. Just the thought of that brings me to tears.

I found myself doing full make-up for the call. As I was putting it on, I thought to myself, What the hell am I doing this for? Its FaceTime, not BBC 1. My sister commented on my strong eye; she clearly thought I was a massive dick for bothering. Personally, I enjoyed looking at it. And that's the thing with those calls, isn't it? You have to stare at your own face too, so you might as well look nice.

I just got back from a walk with Valentine. It's the only way we can get him to nap in the afternoon. It was SO HOT. I had a mask on and got really stressed out. I couldn't breathe properly. No one was around. I wanted to rip it off and take a long, deep breath, but I imagined someone filming me out of their window and the video of the dishevelled-looking mother ripping off her mask in protest and breathing her corona breath all over the pavement going viral. So I kept it on, despite my inner rebel wanting to live my life my way, and put an end to this nonsense.

There is no time for inner rebels right now. We just have to do what we have to do and hopefully this will pass soon.

I feel like a Neanderthal hunter-gatherer every time I go to a shop. I am the family member sent out into the wild to provide for my family. I fight anyone who comes within six feet of me, my breath heavy underneath my mask. My fangs foaming as I select my hummus. I can hear that David Attenborough-inspired voiceover again:

'As the mother of the species makes her way through the aisles with her antibodies, she panics as the regular ingredients are not on the shelves. Her capacity to think fast means she rewrites her menu plans at lightning speed. Ensuring a solid selection of meals and snacks are in her trolley, ready to satisfy her hungry youth who won't flee the nest for another FIFTEEN YEARS. A fact that makes her scream WHAT THE ACTUAL FUCK at the dairy fridge.'

Today, I needed to get stuff from Target. Target is massive and sells everything. It's cheap, but you always spend a fortune because even if you only go for loo roll, you come out with 40,000 useless items that you'll never use. When I arrived, there was a huge line of people waiting to go in. Everyone with masks on. No one daring to look at each other in case

Covid-19 can be transmitted by eye contact. I HATE IT. After I had done a supermarket-sweep-style shop and got all of my non-essentials, I got told off at the till because the front of my trolley was too close to the lady in front. It took everything I had not to scream 'IT ISN'T SNEEZING ON HER.' But I know it's wrong to be remotely shitty with staff who are out there in this pandemic. I politely pulled back my trolley. Then swore violently and silently under my disguise.

I am so excited for a weekend. No work, loads of guilt-free TV and cocktail hour is NOON.

Love Dawn x

12 May
Isolation Update – 'Covid Toe'

DISCLAIMER: I am extremely hungover after Mother's Day and the quality of my writing may be in jeopardy. Also in crisis are my already questionable parenting skills, and my inability to stay out of the fridge.

On Friday my pets offered us the kind of entertainment that lockdown dreams are made of. As Art and I were lying on the bed stroking Lilu, I noticed multiple fleas jumping off her. Upon closer inspection, I realised she was ridden with the blood-sucking criminals (good name for a band). Art and Valentine were fascinated. As they both had nits a few months ago, we all knew what to do, and I got the nit comb that I have for their hair and started dragging the little sods off Lilu. Guys, they kept on coming. Every time I ran the comb through her fur, I caught multiple bugs. POOR LILU. No wonder she's been so annoying lately. Not only must she have been so itchy, but she has a terrible flea allergy. When she gets a bite, it goes bald and sore and scabby. GROSS. I have to be really on top of her treatments and, because her allergy is so bad, the vet recommends her taking the pills, rather than using the topical stuff that goes on the back of her neck. This is all well and good, but she always pukes up the pills. GROSS. Last time she did this, I called the vet to tell him. He asked how long she'd kept the pill down for and I told him about an hour. He thought that was probably enough for it to work. But obviously it wasn't. So poor Lilu had about two months' worth of fleas on her. EXTRA GROSS. I felt bad, I have been so distracted that poor Lilu has been at the bottom of my list and now she's suffering. I have to do better for her. Poor pussycat.

I'd just got the boys a new bug-catching kit, so they loved looking at the fleas through the magnifying glass. I pulled thirty-six off her. THIRTY-SIX. She was immediately happier. I mean, of course she was – can you imagine how annoying they must have been? When I'd got a load off, I gave her another pill and, as per usual, she puked it up. This time only twenty minutes later, so I was sure she hadn't digested it. I needed to get the topical treatment, which, conveniently, I could pick up from the vet later that day because I already had an appointment for Potato at 3 p.m.

Chris had taken the boys and Potato to the park that morning, and all was well. But when they got back, we noticed Potato was being very strange. Obviously in real pain, unable to turn his neck to the left, and he seemed so so sad. He was walking strangely and staring at the ground. It was very unusual for him. He's old now, somewhere between twelve and fourteen, probably. But he is spritely and often mistaken for a puppy, so we forget he's an old man. I squeezed him and he did a little yelp when I touched his neck, so I booked an appointment right away.

It all worked out well. Valentine fell asleep in the car and the vet came out to get Potato. He was in there for about twenty minutes before I got a call to tell me what was wrong with him. Poor Potato has a condition called 'Cervical Disc Disease'. It's basically swelling in his spine around his neck. He was given anti-inflammatory drugs and painkillers, enough for two weeks. After that, we can see how it goes, but he might need them forever. For this two-week period, he is to have no walks and must be very careful. POOR SPUDDY. He was so sad. I took him home to Chris, because Chris is the love of Potato's life, and he administered his first dose. Soon after there was a visible improvement. But the drugs make him really sleepy, so it's all a bit quiet for Potato right now. I'm grateful it happened now, while we are all home to take care of him. I hate it though, the nicest living thing in the entire world in pain. It's just not fair.

Anyway, I highly recommend giving your cat fleas if you need something to do with your kids. Hours of fun.

My sense of taste still isn't great after corona. I spend so long adding flavour to dishes, but most things are still a little bland. I know they taste good because of Chris's sex noises (at dinnertime, because of my cooking – he doesn't just make random sex noises). Also, remember I told you a while ago that I had a terrible toe? I mean it's so gross to even talk about it, but one of my toes blistered up and got really sore. I thought it was heat rash. GUYS, IT WAS 'COVID TOE'. A legit thing that happens a week or so after you've had the virus. I wish I'd never googled it because I now have some visuals that are not helping my hangover, but it's mad to realise what it was. I still can't believe I had coronavirus. It's the most surreal feeling. To think how differently it could have gone. I feel so, so lucky. Sending love to you and yours and hoping everyone you love is safe and well.

Chris and I lay in bed chatting tonight and I had my first real 'OH FUCK' corona moment. What if they don't find a vaccination for a few years? Worse still, what if they don't find one? I got consumed with the idea that life will never be the same again, and then couldn't sleep for hours. By the time I woke up I was a lot calmer about the whole thing, with my usual 'what will be will be, there isn't much we can do about it' attitude. It was also Mother's Day[1] and Chris presented me with a croissant the size of my head. The most perfect distraction from global devastation.

Art is at the age where he fires questions at you but doesn't really care about your answers. The most common one is 'What is your favourite dinosaur?' When he sees me roll my eyes for the fifteenth time that day, he mixes it up a bit and chucks a flurry of new questions like 'What is your third favourite dinosaur?' Or 'What is your favourite carnivore dinosaur?' Followed by 'What is your third favourite carnivore

[1] Mother's Day is later in the US, in May (although who the hell knows what days or months mean any more. Is it Christmas yet?)

dinosaur?' And so on and so on. I'm considering taking more showers throughout the day. He often follows me in and continues with the questions, but the pouring water really helps muffle the sound of his voice. During one of my long, Mother's Day showers he ran in and yelled, 'It's weird that trees have a brown stem and flowers have a green stem.' Then ran off before I had the chance to say anything.

I miss talking about cock with my girlfriends.

My only prerequisite for Mother's Day was that I didn't have to cook anything. And I didn't. It was lovely to be out of the kitchen for a day, despite how much I enjoy it. It did mean that the kids had pizza again, and that I got drunk and can't remember putting them to bed, and that now I feel like I slept in a field with a herd of cows, but it was all totally lovely and worth it. It's so awful waking up with such a hangover though. I felt like I could puke into my bra at any moment and lay on the bed quivering into a cup of tea all afternoon.

The mosquitos are SO bad. Poor Art looks like he's got chick-enpox. I am using the DEET spray, despite the health warnings. Otherwise they eat us alive. But if I forget, we are lunch. I also have the Avon Skin so Soft, and sometimes we wear special bracelets that apparently keep them away. But it's annoying, and exhausting. It's a very new phenomenon here; when I first moved to LA there weren't any. Apparently, a massive nest of them came over on a boat from Egypt and the little fuckers multiplied at a billion times per second and now the whole city is infested. HOW will we ever get rid of them? Or is this just it now? Attacked by the air every time you step outside. Brilliant, just what we all needed on top of the pandemic. But we must be grateful that they don't transmit coronavirus, because if that was the case then we'd all be in bunkers underground, and you can fuck that with two kids under six.

Valentine wet himself three times today. For no other reason than he just couldn't be bothered to move. I can't go back to potty training. Two days ago, he pooed in the pool. He had a full-body rash guard on, so I had to peel it off then take the poo out, put it in the toilet, then wipe his whole body clean. So next time you ask me about my glamorous Hollywood life, please refer back to that visual for details.

Oh, something nice we did. The boys picked the ripe lemons from the lemon tree and we made lemonade. Isn't that dreamy? I felt like such an America Mom while I did it, but it was really nice. This is how we made it . . .

Heat ¾ cup of sugar and a cup of water on the stove until the sugar dissolves
Squeeze enough lemons to make a cup of juice
Mix it all together then add about 3 cups of water
Pour over ice and drink

LOVELY! Try it next time you have some lemons. I also recommend putting vodka in it. Ideally, just yours, unless the kids are being real assholes that day, then just give it to them too.

Potato seems happier now the meds have kicked in. What is sweet is he keeps jumping up to snuggle up to Art. It's quite new, like he's finally realised Art is on his side, and not a terrorist who chases him around the house trying to catch him by the tail. I know I moan, but there is an awful lot of cuteness happening in my house right now. My babies and my furry babies coming together. Just such a shame they all smell of wee.

OK, I have to go and give the kids dinner. I am counting the minutes to bedtime.

Sending you lots of love,

Dawn x

My Daughter and my First-Born Son: Lilu and Potato

As you've probably gathered from these entries, there's been a whole lot of piss, shit and puke generated by the family pets during lockdown. It's like we've been living in a zoo (and that's even without Lilu and Potato), not to mention all the horrible beasties thrown in (no, YOU just thought you saw another cockroach). But animals always bring such comfort and love, and I wouldn't change it for the world. I think my need for pets is as much a part of me as my need for food. I love them SO much.

When I was growing up, my aunt and uncle's pets were extremely important to me. One dog, a beautiful bearded collie called Acre, who used to run away (I refuse to take that personally), was my best friend for a long time. When Jane and I lived with our grandparents, we'd go and stay with Jane and Tony (aunt and uncle) at the weekends. They had two dogs, Acre and Sniff (a border collie), and two Siamese cats, Tiku and Ninn. I was obsessed with them all. My grandparents weren't pet people, so when the weekend arrived, I was always desperate for some furry love. Jane and Tony also had ducks, geese, a tortoise and four beehives. For me, it was an extremely exciting place to be.

Acre though, she was my emotional support animal. I'd been through a lot with my mum dying, and Acre, as far as I could tell, was the only person who really understood me. I'd spend hours and hours down at the beach with her. I'd tell her everything, and she'd lie down so I could use her as a pillow. She licked me and cuddled me and lost her mind when I walked into a room because she was so excited I was there. It was everything I needed at that time in my life. I loved all of Jane and Tony's pets (I was a bit dubious about the bees but accepted their role in the family) but Acre, she was my first love.

I then moved on to the cats, specifically Ninn. She was a seal point Siamese and would lie on my chest and rub her cheeks on mine. She had no teeth, but was amazing at saving me from big spiders in my room. I'd hold her up to them and she'd grab them in her mouth, then suck them to death for me as only a real friend could. Dogs and cats were such a huge part of my upbringing, there was no way I wasn't getting a pet of my own as soon as I felt old enough.

I've had Lilu, my Siamese cat, since I was twenty-four. That's my entire adult life, being responsible for something other than me. That's a pretty big deal. My uncle begged me not to do it. He warned me of the responsibility, saying I'd never be able to go on holiday. That I'd kill the poor thing by forgetting to feed it. That vet bills were huge. That I'd feel trapped and end up giving her away to an old lady down the street. But I was determined. That love I had from Acre and Ninn needed to be replaced. I wanted it again, and I was willing to sacrifice anything, including £300. Which was at the time, and still is, a lot of money.

Now I'd never have a pet that I didn't rescue from a shelter, but all that time ago all I wanted was another seal point Siamese. I'd grown up with them, and loved their complicated, bitchy and emotional personalities. I researched and found a breeder in Hastings, who said that they had a litter due any day. The Internet was still a bit of a mystery at that point, and I never trusted that there were actual people on the other end of websites. But one day, I found myself on the way down to Hastings on the train to choose my kitten.

When I got to the house, the smell of cats hit me immediately. There was a husband and wife and three kids, all of whom were smoking. The husband barely looked up from the enormous TV that nearly blew my socks off when I saw it. And the wife took me to the kitchen to see the kittens. There were six of them; they looked like hands.

I cuddled a few, toyed with the idea of a boy because the lady told me how loyal they were, but then I spotted Lilu. She was all awkward, with a big bend in her tail. I picked her up and she scratched me, but I just knew she was my cat. I sat with her for an hour, watching TV with all the smoking kids, then said goodbye. I'd be able to pick her up in around three weeks. I paid them a £100 deposit.

As I came away on the train I knew I'd done the right thing. I had around £350 in my bank account that would cover the cat and train fees. I'd been saving up for a stereo, but as I lived in a flatshare with seven boys, all of whom had stereos, I chose the cat instead. We didn't need more music.

Back in London I got all the things. A litter tray, little bird toys, catnip, food and flea stuff. By the time I went back for her, I was ready. I'll never forget bringing her home. Sitting on the train with this overwhelming feeling that I was responsible for this tiny thing's life. That without me, she would die.

That I had to grow up really fast, or my uncle was going to be right. The train pulled into a stop, God knows where, and a young guy got on with a pet rabbit.

'Is that a rabbit?' I asked him.

'Yes, is that a kitten?'

'Yes,' I told him.

We sat on the train with his pet rabbit and my pet kitten and talked about how we were going to take them everywhere with us for their whole lives. When we got to London, we said goodbye and pushed the two cases close so that Lilu and his rabbit could sniff noses. It was all very cute and extremely weird. If it had been a movie, we probably would have got married.

I ordered a taxi when I got to London Bridge station, and it took ages to come so I took Lilu to the pub and ordered a beer. The guy on the door kept staring at me. He was a big chap, didn't look like an animal guy. He came over and I thought he was going to say she wasn't allowed in, but instead he yelled, 'FUCK ME, IS THAT A CHIHUAHUA?'

Siamese cats are weird. I knew instinctively I had just purchased a £300 cat that most people would be rude about. I didn't care, I loved her with every inch of my soul.

Lilu and I have travelled the world together. I've remained completely dedicated. Even my uncle admits I've done a good job. There have been periods of time where I wasn't able to look after her myself and have relied on friends to help me. This has gone both well and terribly. A Siamese is a very particular type of cat. She doesn't just sleep in corners and pop her head up for food. She is loud, demanding and wants to be with you. When she gets stressed, she sounds like a screaming baby. She pees on things. She pukes and poos on the floor. You have to really love cats to take care of an animal like Lilu, and some people I have relied on have absolutely hated her. I've had flatmates who didn't get it at all. In one, I had to keep her litter tray in my bedroom. It's fair enough, for some people a litter tray in the bathroom is awful and I didn't argue it. But obviously having it by your bed is even worse. We moved. It's been, at times, extremely stressful, but I have always done my best. If she was somewhere that wasn't working out, I would get her out of there quickly. One time she was in LA while I had to go back to London for work for a few months. I weighed up the stress of flying her internationally and thought she'd be better off at home with a friend. It didn't work out. They did not like each other. The friend kept Lilu in the laundry room and she howled at the top of her lungs to get out. The neighbours complained. Another friend had gone round and told me about it then kindly helped me get Lilu out of America and on a plane to London to be with me. An expense I had been trying to avoid but was happy to do when it needed to be done. I realised then that Lilu was just always better off with her mummy. And since then, I've done a pretty good job of keeping her with me and it's been really lovely. Mostly. She is a massive pain in the ass, but she's got a good heart. We think. Sometimes. Maybe.

I love Lilu so much. Like, so much more than I should love something that has kept me awake more than my children and literally drenched my house in piss. But taking care of her has been one of the greatest joys of my life. My longest relationship. My most consistent love. The other heartbeat when I was alone. She's seen me at my best and worst, and for that reason I'd take the terrible meow any day, because if that cat could talk . . .

The first time I brought Chris home, she tried to sabotage it immediately. He'd stayed the night and things had gone well (AYE AYE WINK WINK), so the next night he stayed too. But when we got home from dinner, Lilu had puked on his side of the bed. Chris was suitably horrified and I was pretty shocked myself. It seemed very deliberate. She clearly knew I liked him and that this interloper was a potential threat to our perfect little life together. But I'm happy to say that these days, they get on very well. Chris likes to pretend he doesn't love her, but I often walk in on them having a cuddle, and he relentlessly buys her beds. I've had to ban her from the bedroom at night because she keeps me awake, but Chris tries to sneak her in. Something about her bitchiness is a challenge; once you crack her and she shows you love, it can be quite addictive.

And then there is Potato. OH POTATO. The sweetest, most loving, cuddliest, kindest, softest most loyal dog. Even my parents, who have said on repeat for most of my life, 'we hate small dogs', adore Potato. He isn't actually that small. More medium-sized. He's a mix of a few things but looks a lot like a Parson Terrier, basically a tall Jack Russell with Dalmatian spots and actual eyebrows.

Chris and I adopted him a year into our relationship, and we really shouldn't have done it. Our relationship was fine, but not particularly stable at that early stage. He'd moved into my flat in LA, and him and Lilu were getting on well. I was unemployed and a bit depressed, and I really wanted a dog. There was a pet shop close to our flat that did adoptions, so I convinced Chris that fostering was a good idea. He was on the fence.

We went to the shop to have a look. I immediately fell in

love with a little scruffy thing that was cute and cuddly. Chris went to stroke it and it tried to bite him. Not the one. And then – and honestly this is how I remember it – Potato ran along a beam of sunlight that ran the length of the shop floor, and straight into Chris's arms. Pretty much where he has been ever since.

We were only supposed to foster, but anyone who knows Potato knows that could never happen. Every Saturday I was supposed to take him back to the shop for the adoptions, and every week I would tell the lady that I thought I had found an owner, and we would be spending the day with them at the beach. This went on for a number of weeks. By this time, the love was real. But we knew we really shouldn't have a dog. I was already broke and financially responsible for a cat. If we kept the dog, it had to be Chris's decision. One Saturday, we decided we would have to take him back. Chris said he would do it, I was too sad. I went for a walk. As I came towards the shop, I saw Chris on the phone outside. He was in deep conversation. He was talking to a friend of his who had a dog, and the friend said to Chris that all we had to do was give the dog a better life than it had now. Chris agreed he could do that. As I approached, he hung up, looked at me and said, 'Let's go get our boy.' Dear Reader, WE ADOPTED HIM. It was magical – even if he was insane at first. He had the worst separation anxiety and screamed so loud when we went out that the neighbours left horrible notes under the door. He pulled the skirting board off the walls and tore down the curtains. But we got him through it. We loved him and trained him and got his confidence to a point where we could all live our lives. And him and Lilu cuddled. They actually cuddled. Adopting Potato was the greatest thing we ever did.

And yes, we have two children but I am not re-writing that sentence.

The pets LOVED lockdown. Having us home all day every day was all they ever wanted. Also, the kids bonded with them in a way they hadn't before. One night, I thought Art would be sleeping as it was well past 9 p.m., but then I went into his room I found him sitting up cuddling Potato, just like I would have done with Acre when I was his age. I imagined Art having that same feeling I experienced: that your dog is your best friend and there for you no matter what.

Valentine is still quite a way from that and terrorises both Lilu and Potato by chasing them around. But I do keep finding him in Lilu's bed with his head on her. She's such a bitch of a cat, but she's never raised a claw to the kids. She knows she has to put up with them, and she does it with total grace. She's a nice person really. Sometimes.

Now I am done with having kids, my need for more pets is growing. Chris has said that I can have a giant tortoise when we move house. Art wants to call it Shelly. Val wants a fish[1].

I don't mind what we get, as long as they love cuddles.

[1] UPDATE: We have since acquired a little yellow fish called Hippo. He was a birthday present for Valentine but remains on my desk because I absolutely adore him. He's not hugely into cuddles, but I'm working on it.

PIECE TEN

Let's Get Spiritual

13 May
Isolation Update – A sober kind of drunk

I'm done with brushing everything off as a coincidence now. Signs are being sent to me from all angles, and I am reading them loud and clear.

I did a Peloton this morning. I didn't realise it, but the class I selected was a Mother's Day theme. My favourite instructor, Ally Love, opened it by saying 'It's Mother's Day' and then she played 'Uptown Girl' by Billy Joel, which is the song that reminds me of my mum the most. Of all the songs, on all the days. The song that reminds me most of my mum, on MOTHER'S DAY. WHAT? This, 'Be Kind' being written in the sky above my house, Valentine suddenly deciding that all of his toys are called 'Carrie'; 2020 came to take me on a deeper and more spiritual journey, I have no doubt. Too many moments of WHAT THE FUCK have come my way to brush them all off as random chance. I keep being sent signs that connect to me to the people I have lost, simple as that. Maybe it's because of my crystals. Let me explain.

A few months ago when I returned to London, I purchased some crystals. I associate them with loss and friendship, because I got them the week of Caroline's funeral. My friend Josie talked me into getting some the day before the funeral. Josie took me to a shop on Broadway Market called 'She's Lost Control' that sold nothing but crystals and told me to pick out the ones I felt drawn to. I felt silly and self-conscious but did it anyway. Because, if I'm honest, I was so heartbroken that I was willing to try anything that promised me a chance of surviving my grief. We later went to a full moon gong bath. A very unusual thing for me to do indeed. But I suppose that is what grief does, if you allow it to: it fundamentally changes you, maybe for the better. It was me, Josie, Ophelia and our friend Camilla. We were all extremely emotional and weepy, and the evening was powerful but sad all at once. At the start, no one was really talking, until the woman next to Josie suddenly piped up and said, 'Hello, my name is Caroline.' WHAT? Anyway, back to the crystals. I was first drawn to one called Labradorite. Upon picking it up and feeling it, and telling Josie that I liked its dark colour, I read the description:

> *A stone that helps us to unleash our creativity and tap into our inner wisdom. Labradorite connects us to our inner mystic and opens up the realms of knowing., that little niggle that we too often ignore. It also gives us the courage to let our creativity flow.*

I immediately felt connected to it. Grief had terrified me in terms of being creative. I couldn't think of anything else, not even for a second. I realise it was all very new, but I couldn't imagine a day where I had the focus to write anything ever again. I had moments where I presumed my career was over, that I'd have to just stop. How could I ever talk about anything but the devastation I was experiencing? It was a feeling that was consuming me as much as the sadness itself – the fear that the part of me that was able to create had died too. How could I ever be funny again? It felt so wrong to even try. This stone gave me a glimmer of hope. I held it tight in my hand and headed for the till. On the way over, another one caught my eye. This time a whiter rock, with an orange glow. Citrine. I read the description:

> *Citrine is known as the stone of success, promoting energies of fortune and luck. Wearing Citrine will attract love and happiness and open the mind to new ideas. It radiates confidence and power, and uniquely doesn't store any negativity, instead leaving room for happiness.*

As you can imagine, I grabbed it and held it close. These were my crystals. I had no need to look around the shop. I found the ones I was supposed to find. I was later to discover that Citrine is Caroline's birthstone – November. I chose to take that as a sign that this was the stone for me, and I have slept with it under my pillow ever since.

The truth is, despite grief and Covid presenting me with a wall that I couldn't get over, I have found myself to be excessively creative since the crystals came into my life. I keep them close to me. I talk to them and thank them and I tell them that I'm glad they're here. When I cry, I hold them. They make me feel like my best friends are in my hands. I love them.

I have no desire for more. My house doesn't need to be full of them, I don't need to hang them around my neck. But this simple relationship that I have with these two is important to me.[1] They represent a lot. They make me feel nice. So that's just that.

I was wondering about what else I have learned about myself during lockdown, other than that I am way more spiritual than I am willing to admit, and one thing that has become very apparent is that, no matter how hard I try to be, I am not an alcoholic. Turns out, I'm the kind of drunk who wants to experience life sober. Also, I have itchy skin and lower back pain which is ABSOLUTELY a cry for help from my kidneys to give them a break. Luckily, gummies have a vastly different effect on your insides, so I have zero plans to slow my consumption of those. ALSO, they make me a better mum (LA LA LA, I'm not listening). ALSO, Chris literally just walked in and put a glass of rosé on my desk. One more for the road? Fuck it. (Still, not an alcoholic.)

OH, one huge revelation from today was that I brushed my hair. I haven't brushed my hair, when dry, for nearly fifteen years. I have convinced myself that if I do, it will go frizzy. Turns out, it doesn't go frizzy, it just looks really nice. So now I am a marginally sober woman with crystals and long brushed hair. WHO EVEN AM I?

1 UPDATE: Since writing this I have purchased two Citrine bracelets. Turns out, they make me feel like Caroline is with me. One of them, however, is somewhere in the Pacific Ocean. Valentine yanked it and stretched it, which meant it was loose. We all went to the beach and as I jumped over a wave, the bracelet flew off. I was so sad at first, but then imagined Caroline jumping in the waves and thought she'd be quite happy to have a swim in the Pacific Ocean. So, I gently mouthed, 'enjoy the water, my love' and was happy to let it go.

OK, that's it from me tonight. In a day where I thought nothing happened, my emotions ran high. So lovely to have a place to write about it at the end of the day.

Tell me about your day, your crystals, and your hair.

Love Dawn x

14 May
Isolation Update – Am I eighty yet?

It's so bizarre that I am being positive about crystals, when for most of my life I have actively turned away from anyone who mentions them. I'm enjoying being honest about the calm they offer me and feel delightfully un-silly about it. Do you ever imagine your 24-year-old self seeing your 41-year-old self and thinking, 'YOU ARE SUCH A DORK'? I do. But who cares, my 41-year-old self looks at my 24-year-old self and thinks 'YOU'RE SUCH A DESPERATE WANNABE.' I don't think they would get along at all. Best keep them apart.

I've always been happy to get older and found my younger years very easy to put behind me. I was on a desperate quest for success, I was always trying to be liked, I was loud and determined to be noticed, I was uncomfortable, off my head and far too slutty. At the time it was all fun and games. I thought nothing of staying up all night doing God knows what, then rolling into my job at a TV production company having had not a wink of sleep, my eyes rolling in my head, stinking of fags, and barely being able to say my own name, let alone make television. That was how my early twenties were. It was fun. In my opinion, exactly how it should have been. But to be doing that again now, no. I have no interest in all that.

I've never been scared of getting old. My gran lived until she was eighty-six and was cute as a button – I want to be like that. My aunty Jane, now eighty-three, is everything I want to be. She is so smart, so fit, so active. She may be a little slower, but you'd never guess her age. I find her so inspiring, and if I get the chance to be like my aunty Jane, I'll make the most of every second. I think women get better with age; being an old lady has always appealed to me. I guess that is what happens when you have good ones around you. I long for my future. I am excited for it. So far, I like what age has done to my head, my face, my body and my relationships. I like age because it means I'm still alive. I can't wait to see what I'm like when I'm seventy. Will I still be wearing these clothes? Probably. Will I still be writing stuff down? Definitely. Will I live in a house with small children in it? NO, I WILL NOT.

I will be free of so many things. I hope I'll be healthy enough to enjoy it.

I was thinking. You know in January when you bump into people for the first time after Christmas and you ask how their Christmas was and by about 14 January you're thinking, SERIOUSLY, how long do we have to ask this for? Well, what do you think it will be like after the pandemic? How long will we have to ask how everyone's lockdown was before we can just shut the hell up about it and move on? I'm guessing YEARS. So many, many years.

My neighbour is building an extension. The drilling and banging is destroying me from the inside. But it's not only the noise, it's the lack of privacy. There are three guys on a roof, who can see directly into our garden all day. That, AND the drilling is so intense. Earlier, both of my kids were yelling 'SHUT UP, MAN' at them, and I just went inside and didn't tell them to stop. Is that terrible? I mean, the men can't stop, they have a job to do, but who am I to tell my kids not to speak their minds?

I LOVE my neighbour, so this isn't the kind of issue where I'm going to be a bitch about it, but MY GOD, what a brutal time to sort your extension out. Finding any kind of peace or quiet during the day is impossible. They start at 7 a.m., same time as the kids. The workmen leave at 4 p.m., but the kids go on until 8 p.m. By then I am broken. AND WE WONDER WHY I DRINK?

Also, we have no right to complain. Our renovation continues around ten minutes away on the new house and I'm sure our new neighbours feel the same way. It's running months over and so stressful. I am so excited to move house and so grateful that it's coming, but my God, they are not kidding when they say it's stressful. SO many things to decide.

I went to the shops to buy food. I got pâté. I didn't go out for it, but I came home with it. ISN'T THAT EXCITING???

THAT'S IT FROM ME.

Until tomorrow,

Love Dawn x

15 May
Isolation Update – open wide

You know those crystals I was talking about and how I sleep with them under my pillow? I might put them in my mouth tonight and hope for a miracle.

At around 2 a.m. we were woken up because Valentine was in the hallway trying to open the living room door. He wasn't happy about the fact that he couldn't do it. 'WAHHHHH, I CAN'T OPEN THE DOOR,' he yelled, on repeat, for quite some time.

Luckily for me, though, my wonderful husband has always been amazing about getting up with the kids in the night, and before I'd even had the chance to take out my earplugs, remove my eye mask and gently slide off my silk turban, Chris had Valentine in his arms and was taking him back to bed. I popped an extra melatonin and went back to sleep, only to discover in the morning that Chris had lain with Val for an hour before he went back to sleep. I felt awful. My turn tonight, if Val decides to do another random walk down the hallway in pitch-darkness for absolutely no fucking reason at all.

I have a fried egg on toast pretty much every morning, does anyone else? I bloody love eggs. My dream would be to have chickens and go get fresh ones every morning. We actually wanted to get some for our new house, but apparently the rules in California are that the chickens have to be at least thirty feet from your neighbours. We can't because the houses on our new street are very close together. BUMMER. One day . . . one has to have a dream.

There was a lizard in our garden today. It was so cute. I'd laid out a rug for the boys to have a picnic on and it just planted itself right in the middle of it. Obviously, Valentine wanted to put it in his sandwich and kept thrusting at it, so the poor little lizard was terrified. It froze, wondering if these three massive monsters were going to eat it. Eventually he realised that wasn't going to happen (literally had to hold Valentine back) and scuttled off into the bushes. How joyous. For a while there we sat and ate while he watched us. It was particularly funny as he was right next to the kids' toy lizards and I really think he was confused. I mean, you would be. It's a bit like when you're in a shop and there's a mannequin behind you and it makes you jump because you think it's a person standing dangerously close. Then, after some amount of time – sometimes not much, sometimes a lot – you realise it's not an axe murderer and continue to finger the blouses.

I hope we see more lizards because my kids were entranced for the entire time it sat with us. Of course, we could get a pet lizard. But Valentine would let it go and it would find its way into my bed and nibble my Covid Toe in my sleep. I can't be having that on top of EVERYTHING ELSE.

It's 15 May tomorrow. The date that lockdown was supposed to lift. But it isn't lifting, and very little will change. Certain things will lighten up. Small groups may be OK. Childcare is becoming acceptable and I am IN. More restaurants will do take out. You can play golf and buy some flowers, but the world is still fucked. We're in this for the long haul, that is just how it is.

But you know, I think lockdown has been good for me. Chris and I are so bad at taking holidays, we just never did. We'd go for very occasional weekend breaks, but rarely anything more. Usually Chris's job means he's away a lot, so just being at home with nowhere to go (OH THE IRONY) was generally enough of a break for us. For this reason, we were tired before this started. Exhausted, even. We'd both worked so hard for a few years, with no proper breaks. With the kids, weekends were harder work than the nine-to-five. We love our work, so it's generally OK, but we really needed some time to take it easy.

Actually, I wouldn't say looking after Art and Valentine during lockdown has been taking it easy, but not having deadlines and pressure, and work-related travel and long filming hours, and dealing with separation has been lovely. Creatively, I was really struggling for words earlier this year. I felt like I'd written all of my ideas, and that I'd totally burnt out. NOT ANY MORE. I am now raring to go. My creative juices are shooting out of me like jizz flying up the walls. I am JIZZING IDEAS all over the house. A quick book jizz in the kitchen, a blog jizz in the garden, a huge podcast jizz all over the living room. It feels really, really good to be excited by my own thoughts again. Woo-hoo to a house that's splattered with jizz.

I got into bed tonight and gave my crystals an extra squeeze then tucked them back under my pillow. I feel very protective of them. They are literally the last things I want to get jizz on.

Why do I keep talking about jizz? I need to sleep.

Sending you all of my love, and hope you're all OK,

Love Dawn x

Who even am I, Mystic Meg?

I've never really believed in anything. Quite the opposite, actually. I have, at times, seen religion or spirituality as a weakness. Why would people need to believe in something they couldn't prove, when they could just believe in the reality of their own existence? All I ever heard from people who believed in things, was that they were on a constant mission of self-improvement. It all felt so exhausting. Why can't they just accept their flaws and get on with it? Who were they trying to be perfect for? I never understood it. I felt people leaned towards spirituality when they couldn't cope. I'd get enormously judgemental about it, because personally I'd rather bury all my feelings and have them play out in weird and destructive ways than ever go through a process of trying to sort them out.

I did have an experience of sorts about eight years ago. Funnily enough, I was with Caroline on Melrose Avenue in LA. We wandered into a fortune teller's shop which, by some weird chance, backs on to the house I live in now. Caroline and our friend Gemma Cairney, who had come to stay with me for a while, both wanted to get readings. I, of course, thought the whole thing was utterly ridiculous. While they sat in the corner with the main lady – who I need only describe as looking like a fortune teller, because she looked exactly as you'd expect one to look – I stood twiddling my thumbs in the middle of a room. Suddenly, another woman appeared out of nowhere and sat me down on the couch. Before I knew it she was looking at my hand. 'Hmmmm,' she said. 'Your life line isn't very long.'

'Great,' I huffed. 'Anything else?'

'Hmmm, yes. You'll be having a miscarriage or an abortion.'

She then stood up and walked away. I was obviously stunned.

'How much do I owe you?' I called after her. To which she replied, 'Don't worry about it,' before disappearing behind a curtain.

'Did anyone else even see her?' I asked the room. No one confirmed that they did.

Later that day, Gem and Caroline and I were in the back of a taxi. We were all very hungover, and Gem was threatening to be sick. We were all very hot and bothered and in terrible moods. After a long spell of silence, and quite unprompted, I said, 'I can't wait for my abortion.' At which Caroline erupted with the kind of laughter that would stop traffic, and Gemma threw up.

Thankfully, I never had a miscarriage, and neither did I choose to have an abortion. I considered my faith in anything spiritual well and truly dashed after that. I still have no idea if that woman even worked there.

But then 2020 happened.

Soon after Caroline died, I felt entirely connected to the idea that she was still with me. The sheer impossibility that she had gone was not something I could grasp. I lay on my back in the middle of the garden, looked up at the clouds and said the words, 'OK, Universe, I'm listening. Talk to me.'

And so it did. First up, it had a plane write the words 'Be Kind' right above my head. I still can't believe that happened. Anyway . . .

A week before she died, I had been asked to be godmother to my friends Jonny and Michelle's baby girl. As I have two boys, it was emotional as they 'gave me a girl'. I was so honoured. They asked me if I was sure about the responsibility, of which I had no doubt. There was just one issue: as I was never christened myself, I'm not legally allowed to be a godmother. I know, I know, I can feel the devil calling my name too, but they didn't mind about that, which was such a relief. So, I became the loving, unofficial but entirely dedicated godmother to a perfect little chunky-thighed dollop of deliciousness called Phoenix. Hi, Phoenix, if you are now grown up and I am making you read all of my old books, I love you very much.

Phoenix was an extremely cute baby, and I had big plans to take her for walks and even have her sleep at my house, so Jonny and Michelle could get some rest. But then Caroline died, and I couldn't do it. I couldn't do anything. I felt like my head had been filled with exhaust fumes. I couldn't focus on anything, let alone a baby. And I felt really bad about it. Of course, my friends completely understood. But still, it was a shame. And then I realised something that hadn't immediately been obvious to me. Phoenix was born on 9 November, the same day as Caroline. It hit me like a hundred butterflies flying into my face at once. A big shock, but actually rather lovely when you stop trying to shoo them away. At the time,

I was willing to grab hold of anything that offered me the slightest feeling of comfort. Nothing like a baby to do that.

Then came the tree.

I have never believed that dead people go anywhere. I don't think about heaven or hell: I am here now, and this is my one chance. I'm not to waste it. But when Chris and I moved into our house in LA, a cute three-bedroom bungalow just off the grungy end of Melrose Avenue, long before we had kids, I did nominate a palm tree that I could see out of the bathroom window to be my mum. At the time, I'd obviously been feeling a bit emotional and felt I needed to connect with her in some way. I would stand at the window and say goodnight and good morning. I'd occasionally ask her to help me out and watch over me, if I thought I needed her to. It was nice. I knew it wasn't my mum, it was a tree, but it was a little focus point that I could direct my feelings towards. I liked the tree. It was one of those tall, thin and bendy palm trees that totally defied ergonomics. I remember thinking, 'If you can keep standing tall, so can I, tree.' From my bathroom it was alone in the sky and looked magical.

It's now my kids' bathroom, so I rarely use it or stand there long enough to look at my tree. If I'm honest, I'd forgotten about it for the last few years. But one night recently, as my kids were in the bath, I looked in the mirror at my devastated face and for the first time in years I thought of my mum's tree. I looked out of the window and it was still there, but now it wasn't alone. Another, smaller tree was growing right up alongside it. Where did that come from? An entire tree, just like that? I decided that the new tree was Caroline, and sometimes I go into the bathroom, and I chat to both of them at the same time. It's nice. I recommend nominating trees as people that you have lost, because for the most part they don't go anywhere, they continue to grow, and you can always rely on them to just shut up and let you be sad.

Caroline's funeral didn't happen for a few weeks. That was a long time to be on the other side of the world from my friends, talking to trees. Chris and I were both set to go, but as the time got closer there were rumours about borders being closed and, even though we never truly believed it would happen, we felt nervous to both be in another country from our kids. We didn't have a nanny, so it was already emotionally stressful to be away and leave them with our only regular babysitter. We decided that Chris would stay home, at least then if I got stuck (it would never happen though, right? How could you shut America's borders? Ridiculous!), the kids would be with their dad. Leaving was impossible, but I couldn't not be there for Caroline. Her mum and sister had asked me to say a few words at the service and I was determined, although terrified, to get through it.

I stayed with Josie in her sweet flat by Hackney Fields. It felt so familiar and I couldn't think why. When I told my sister where I was staying, we realised that she had lived in the house next door for years. She knew exactly where I was, she even knew the woman who lived upstairs. I allowed the coincidence to find itself on the list of signs I was being sent, that the big life I live is actually quite tiny, which was a lesson I think I maybe needed to learn.

By the time I got to Josie, we were both cried out. We were like two birds that had just flown into a window, leaving us stunned and trapped in a moment of time that felt endless and impossible to navigate. We talked and talked. Various levels of pain, anger and love peaking and troughing as we freely let ourselves say whatever it was we needed to say. And then Josie said, 'My crystals will protect me.'

Oh here we go, I thought as my eyes did an involuntary roll. I've lost Josie to the madness of crystals.

But for once I couldn't summon up the energy to contest the notion, so rather than scoff, I listened. She went on . . .

'A few months ago, I needed to find somewhere to live, so I asked my crystals for a two-bedroom flat near Hackney Fields, with a bath and garden, for a reasonable price. The next day I was in a taxi and I was telling the driver I needed a place, and he said, "I know somewhere." And he connected me with the woman who owns this flat – and here I am, living in it. It's exactly what I asked for.'

'Where did you get these crystals?' I asked, putting my coat on. And before I could say 'How do you spell amethyst', we were walking down Broadway Market to her favourite crystal shop.

On the way, we walked through London Fields. We were talking about Gemma and I was saying how I couldn't wait to see her. I met Caroline and Gemma at the same time, in Australia. Caroline was host of *I'm a Celebrity Get Me Out of Here Now*, and Gemma and I had been invited down to sit on the panel and discuss the contestants in the jungle. We'd had the most amazing week, bonding for life. I was craving her. As Josie and I entered London Fields, the sun was going down minus one beam of it that was shining directly on the face of someone who was standing alone in the middle of the park. 'Is that Gemma?' Josie said. And it was. We all ran towards each other, the person I had wished for just standing there, the final rays of sunshine bouncing off her cheeks.

'I just stopped to watch the sun go down,' she said.

And I thought, no, that isn't what happened, actually. The universe just made you stand still so we could find each other. That's a much more likely story.

PIECE ELEVEN

And Sleep . . . Or Not

18 May
Isolation Update – How many meals?

I am so beside myself about Trump that I couldn't get to sleep last night. The drinking bleach comments, the hydroxy-chloroquine, the racism, the stupidity, the hair, the face, it is too much. The fear he will get in again in November, and how America will respond. It's frightening, truly. When I eventually fell asleep I had really graphic dreams about all my friends dying. People keep talking about how vivid their Covid dreams are. Mine are also really dark. Maybe I need to start making more vegan dinners? Although I'll miss the cheese.

I need you to know that I did a lot of karaoke this weekend. I had my moments where I could feel myself welling up, but I did manage to enjoy it. Finding songs with no memories attached seemed to do the trick. I have a new song that I am trying to perfect. It's not easy, but I am determined to get it right. It's a lesser known Cher song called 'Just Like Jesse James'. Heard it? Go and listen to it right now. When isolation is over and I am allowed back into karaoke bars, I'm going in strong with that song. It ticks all my boxes. Country vibes with some good crescendo. It will work well with my finger clicks and air punches, my classic moves.

As usual I was drunk for most of the weekend, ate 309,581,239,058 meals and feel like an absolute bloater now, but we got through it so all good. The thumb on my right hand is very sore, and I presume it's from texting so much. This is worrying. If I lose my hands, I lose everything. I need to protect it, but how? I attempted to dictate a few texts, but my phone seems to want to get me into trouble and does not type what I actually say. Also, Chris could hear me bitching to my mates and I didn't feel right about that. I'm not really sure what to do. My thumb needs a break, but I need to be in constant digital contact with everyone I know. So I guess I'm just going to lose the thumb?

We got stoned on Friday afternoon so ate two huge bags of crisps before we ordered a Chinese. None of that is OK, and I couldn't sleep because my tummy hurt so bad. We giggled a lot though and sounded awesome down the microphones for the karoake, so who cares about chronic indigestion and tripling my daily calorie intake in under thirty minutes. I DON'T.

I cut the kids' hair. Valentine looks like he had an operation.

There was a HORRIBLE smell of fish in the kitchen yesterday. It made no sense. I was so scared there was a dead animal somewhere, then Chris discovered an old bowl of Potato's food under the cabinet. He pulled it out and MY GOD, it was FULL of flies and maybe even maggots. HOW can that happen when we are home all the time? I feel shame.

I was getting in a tizz because none of my clothes fit any more, when a late Mother's Day gift from Chris arrived. It's an Anthropologie jumpsuit with a loose waist and it hides ALL of my paunch. I'm never taking it off. Isn't that super? No need to work on my weight because I have an outfit that accommodates it. The perfect solution to what I am going to describe as 'Quarantine Belly'.

We popped down to our new house yesterday. It's coming on great and we really might be in in July[1]. Only a year later than expected. While I was upstairs, out of the window I saw a woman walk up the driveway. She was wearing a purple dressing gown, and my guess would be that she lives in one of the tents around the corner. Tents are a common feature in LA, the homeless problem is at breaking point. It is entirely normal for homeless people to pop up tents on residential and commercial streets. Around where we live, there are a lot. I noticed some a few moments from our new house, and I am guessing this lady lived in one of them. She was probably late sixties and looked all the lovely kinds of bonkers. She had the most radiant smile on her face. She seemed very at home in our garden, which would lead me to believe this wasn't her first visit. She had a plastic bag and a pair of scissors. I wondered if she was coming inside to use a toilet (let's not think about what the scissors were for) as the house is obviously not being lived in right now. I wasn't going to stop her, but was pleased when she headed for the rose bush outside the front door instead. She proceeded to cut the heads off all the roses and put them in her plastic bag.

I probably should have stopped her, but it was nice to watch. The chances are, she doesn't have many things, so who am I to stop her having a few nice flowers to brighten up wherever she was going next? Isn't that exactly what flowers are for? She wandered off after she'd taken what she wanted

[1] We were never going to be in in July, and we weren't. Anyone could have told me that.

and headed down the street into someone else's driveway. When we left, I looked at the bush. Nearly all the roses had been chopped off, so it looked a little sad. Just a green, thorny bush, all its hard-earned blossoms snatched away. Because I am spiritual as fuck these days – seeing signs in everything, sleep with crystals and apparently talk to trees – I went over to the bush and thanked it for being kind. 'I'll take care of you for that,' I said, as I walked away. And I meant it, I will.

It probably wants to stab me with all its thorns for standing by while a well-known local flower snatcher butchered it, but still. The lady's smile stayed with me for the rest of the day. She can have the bush if she wants.

Bye for now.

Love Dawn x

20 May
Isolation Update – Your five-year-old has a big aubergine

Remember how I talked about cooking more vegan dinners? I've just stuffed jasmine rice into a cup, patted it down and turned it upside down to create the most perfect rice mound (anyone else just get a visual of the weird plastic mound between a mannequin's legs?) It's so simple, but looks very impressive, and I am going to go on about it for quite some time. The mannequin's fanny is surrounded by a very delicious vegetarian curry that I can't share the recipe for because I made it up as I went along. I sprinkled chopped spring onions on top, and then Chris had the fantastic idea of putting cashews in it. All in all, we are currently enjoying a highly satisfactory vegan meal. Expect smugness.

Last night I messaged one of the mums from Art's class to check in and see how she was. I don't know her very well, but she's so nice and she's working her ass off with twin boys, so I wanted to show some support. As we were chatting she said something about her little boy not being able to sit down for long, and then I accidentally sent her the aubergine emoji.

She didn't mention it.

It's torturing me.

Did she not notice, or does she think I made a weird joke about her five-year-old's willy?

Why can't there be a spell checker for emojis?

OK, I need to wash up and sleep. Until tomorrow,

Love Dawn x

21 May
Isolation Update – I feel pretty

I cut my fringe and it looks OK. I have to tilt my head a little because it's got a slight wonk to it, but it's good. I might attempt to cut my hair next week, anyone done it yet?

I think I might be ovulating. I say this because I felt pretty today. Has anyone else noticed how that happens? I didn't have a clue about ovulation until I was trying to get pregnant with Art. Why doesn't anyone at school teach you that you can only get pregnant for four to five days a month? Is it just so young girls don't get casual about unprotected sex? If I had known it was THAT hard to get pregnant, I'd have had way more fun. (I'm joking, USE A CONDOM.)

I was fascinated by it all when I wanted to conceive. After a few months in I couldn't work out why I wasn't pregnant. I just thought it would be a case of ditching the birth control, spreading my legs and BAM. But nothing happened. Obviously, the first thought and worry was that I couldn't do it, but then a friend asked me when I ovulate and laughed when I said I had no idea. She explained how reproduction works. 'You release an egg (ovulation) and the sperm has to catch it before it leaves your body.' Simple. Perhaps I thought that there was always an egg floating around. I hadn't listened during sex education at school, because I was too busy scratching cocks into the desks with my compass. Anyway, I worked out when I was ovulating and the next month got pregnant. Fascinating.

(I want to say I realise this is not an easy ride for a lot of people. I was extremely lucky how easily I conceived my first kid, and I don't take that for granted for a single day. I'm sorry if the journey isn't so straightforward for you.)

I also discovered that when you ovulate you produce a thinner mucus than the usual (I REFUSE TO SAY ~~DISCHARGE~~ IN THIS DIARY) so that the sperm can travel more freely to the egg. If you look out for it, you'll see it in your knickers. (Not apologising to the male readers, this is how you were made.) ANYWAY, another thing that happens when you ovulate is that you can feel pretty. Almost like an animal in the wild that fluffs itself up, changes colour or does a weird walk, you are in 'attracting a mate' mode, and mother nature has given you a little dose of self-confidence to get you through it. Isn't that kind of her?

I woke up starving at 5 a.m. Ravenous, in fact. I had to fight the need to get up and make a sandwich. I just don't understand how vegans stay full (I had a vegan dinner, remember?). I really go for it with the nuts or tofu but it's always the same. Starving hours later or in the morning. I really love the idea of a few vegan meals a week, but I can't be dealing with that feeling. Tell me, vegans, I know I have a few of you here, how do you stay full? I need to sleep!

I just ate a peanut butter cup and we are having lamb chops for dinner. My fave.

Love Dawn x

PS I had a dream that we did a massive event and I walked out on-stage singing Cher's 'Just Like Jesse James' and you all joined in. PLEASE can we make that happen when this is all over?

21 May
Isolation Update – Mum, stop scratching your fanny

As you've probably gathered, I'm really not sleeping well at the moment. I lie there for ages having horrible thoughts, and then get really vivid dreams that wake me up in a state. Last night I wandered around the house for hours before I could turn myself off again (did I just describe myself as a Nora Jones lyric?).

Anyway, I think the lack of sleep is making me sad again. I've been very weepy. Last night Chris took over bathtime with the boys so I could just sit outside and have a moment to think. I want space and time to think about Caroline, and that's very hard to get. If real life was happening, I'd take the odd day off work and go sit up a mountain and sob, but that isn't something I can do right now. But to just sit out at the back, alone, for an hour was soooo nice. Although as soon as I went out, a cop helicopter started circling the house. So loud. A little scary. There was a baddy very close. Then Lilu, who never comes out the back, started yelling at me. For NO reason other than to make peace and quiet impossible. Honestly, it's like Caroline keeps throwing things at me every time I try to think about her too much. Like she's saying, 'Don't you dare. Get up, get on with it, don't be sad.' I ended up having a laugh about it, because by the time there was silence it was time to read the kids their stories. OK, OK, I get the hint, Flack!

But it was still nice just to sit there.

Last night, I accidentally made a FANTASTIC lamb pie. Remember I said we were having lamb chops? (Of course you don't, why would you?) WELL, you can imagine my horror when I unwrapped them to reveal DUH DUH DUUUHHHHH, some weird-looking lamb chunks on sticks.

GUTTED. I was so excited for the succulent, crispy fat of a lamb chop. Having the salty juices stream down my chin as I hold one in my mouth, turn to Chris and say, 'Have I got something in my teeth?'

EVERY. TIME.

Alas, it was not to be. I had to think fast, so did this.

Fried an onion, put in about seven whole cloves of garlic. Browned the lamb with some rosemary. Took lamb out. Boiled down a glass of red, some beef stock. Let it simmer and reduce. Put the lamb back in. Tin of tomatoes and a massive spoonful of Bisto gravy granules. Let it simmer an hour. Defrosted some pastry, rolled it out, put the filling in a dish, covered it in pastry, whacked it in the oven, served it with salad, went to bed, GOT LAID.

It was a FUCKING triumph.

I missed people today. My aunty, uncle, dad, sister. When will we be able to fly home to see them? It all seems so impossible. We've invited loads of family for Christmas, but God knows who will come. I realise it's a bit of a funny year, but does anyone else start planning Christmas around now? I always do. I LOVE Christmas and attach a lot to it.

The whole ritual of the day: presents in the morning, a big brunch, the huge turkey, the treats, the drinks, the hats, the passing out in front of the fire. I love big crowds, or small crowds. And I LOVE the food. When Christmas is done well, there is nothing better. When it's done badly, there is nothing worse. I've had a few stinkers, not that I'm not going to go into those, but some Christmas Days make for many happy memories.

My perfect Christmas looks like this.

A big dinner on Christmas Eve. (The perfect dish? Beef Wellington.) On Christmas morning the kids open stockings that we leave in their room. After that, downstairs for breakfast – ham and eggs. Call whatever family are not around with Christmas music blaring in the background. More presents. While the kids play with all their toys, I prep some food and start drinking. Some downtime for everyone around noon. At two, hordes of people arrive for pigs in blankets and whatever hors d'oeuvres I've pulled together. Smoked salmon, vol au vents, the works. At four, we sit down to Christmas dinner. Turkey, ham, maybe even a beef joint with all the trimmings. After that, Christmas pudding (I love it) and something else (because everyone else hates it). Then mountains of Stilton and port. We'd sit at the table for hours chatting, then play games until we are so drunk we can't stand any more. Someone might get a guitar out at this point, and there would definitely be some karaoke. Then into the living room for a movie and too much chocolate. We'd all fall asleep, then wake up and have one more plate of food and a sherry before bed. Or maybe it would all kick off again and we'd play music and sing until we lose our voices. PERFECT.

Oh God, I can taste it all now. I hope we get to spend Christmas with people this year, although I must say, one of my favourites ever was when I was just about to give birth to Art and it was just Chris and me. I was enormous, but cooked a twelve-pound turkey with all the sides and it was SO fun. I wore a huge red kaftan and we had the best day. The idea of just us with the boys in our new house this year isn't so bad.

Valentine is three on 1 July. His last birthday was just the four of us on a beach in Vancouver, so it's sad to think he might not get much more than that again. Not that he has a bloody clue. Yesterday I gave him a cookie for Chris, and he gave it to him while singing 'Happy Birthday'. He just thinks it's a song you sing when you give people sweet things. He also yelled at me this morning for not knowing what his weirdest-looking dino was, and then ran off saying, 'It's my birthday, it's my birthday.' Maybe we shouldn't tell him it's his birthday and just wait until he can have a party? He'd have no idea. Every day is his birthday, as far as he's concerned. Nice attitude, I suppose.

My kids gave me a pedicure nearly three months ago and I still have it. I'm all for keeping up appearances in some ways, but in others I've totally dropped the ball. My nails being one. When I first moved to LA I used to get mani/pedis once or twice a week. I had a brilliant place that charged me $30 for both and I was in and out in an hour. Back then, I only ever wore bright orange and I saw those nails as an extension of my personality. I later moved on to white, which I loved because it felt all sixties. Nails always very short and filed round, never square. That was my look. Since having kids, however, my look is what I like to call 'the mummicure'. It consists of no nail varnish, overgrown cuticles and various uneven lengths. This is largely due to hands being in either washing up or bathwater. Because I got so used to having no varnish on, I quite like my one red foot and one nude foot that the boys did for me. Some nails were only half done, but still, who cares. Also, with my Covid Toe still lingering, what the hell does it matter anyway?

HAVE YOU THROWN UP YET?

I have a mosquito bite right up in my crotch and it's causing me a great deal of stress. I'm worried that, when I've gone, my kids will describe me like this: 'She never stopped singing, wore ridiculous dresses, drank too much and was always scratching her fanny.'

It's not how I want to be remembered.

ANYONE ELSE GOT AN ITCHY FANNY THEY WANT TO TALK ABOUT?

Please don't answer that.

Love Dawn x

22 May
Isolation Update – Godzilla found his way to my knickers again

Earlier this evening, as I was washing my child's hair, I had a strange feeling of unfamiliarity. Washing my children felt like a novel experience, but why? I do this every day, I thought . . . Don't I?

It turns out, I do not.

I realised I hadn't done it since last Wednesday, and even then, there had been no hair washing. They were disgusting. Sticky. This is now how we roll.

Art has dreadlocks. Valentine has developed a fear of cleanliness. I made a Happy Birthday video for my friend, then realised after I had sent it that there was food all over my chest. I used to be better turned out than this. I used to wear clean clothes. I mean, don't get me wrong, I still wear GREAT clothes. They just stink.

I've been shopping for sofas and it's impossible. Why are there so many? Like, if you were going to start any business, wouldn't sofas be the last one you would try? It must be the most saturated market on the planet, right? I mean, I get it, there are loads of us and we all need a place to sit, but Jesus. I am overwhelmed. I just want a nice-looking comfy sofa bed that doesn't cost a million dollars. But they're all SO ugly. And if they're not ugly, they're impractical. And if they're not ugly and impractical then they have weird piping on them, and if they're not ugly, impractical with weird piping on them, then I just HATE THEM. It's such a huge part of your home, isn't it? There's too much choice. Everyone should just be given a free sofa when they are born and have to keep it forever. That would be so much easier. Luck of the draw.

Might just get some bean bags. Maybe if we don't fill our house with furniture, we could just lay rugs down instead, with occasional pouffes and sleep mats. We could squeeze in as many friends as possible and create a commune? Because I don't know if you've noticed but 'WE HAVE A VACCINE

FOR COVID-19' is NOT a sentence I am hearing. What if isolation goes on for months, years, FOR EVER? Honestly, the world has gone so mad this year that I am not ruling out anything. It's time to make plans for permanent lockdown, and it starts here. No sofas and multiple friends moving in. Throw in a wine, tequila and lime juice delivery service and I reckon I could coast like this for years.

I keep watching videos on how to make sourdough bread. I want to make it so badly, but it's SO much effort for a loaf of bread that I can just buy in literally 1/10th of the time. I have enough on my plate (BA BOOM). This is not the time to make very demanding bakery items, is it? But Instagram tells me I should be better at baking. You know what, I successfully made cupcakes a few weeks ago, or wait, was that months ago? What date even is it? I have no idea. What's my name again? Oh yes, bread. I'll get some from the shops tomorrow.

What were we talking about again? Who cares.

My womb has fired up again. Last night I slept badly, because nothing changes there, and was up in raging agony every three hours. I'd take more painkillers, then BAM, three hours later Godzilla found his way back into my knickers and started eating me from the inside out. If that sounded remotely sexy, I can assure you, it wasn't. I have a few more nights of it to go, then I'll be done for a few weeks.

I'd totally forgotten I did it, but I was in so much pain in the night I must have googled alternative remedies and ended up spending $100 on this thing called an Ovira. Has anyone ever heard of it? It's a weird contraption you put on your belly and it sends electrical pulses to your brain telling it you are not actually in pain.

I think we all know I just wasted $100.

What a hideous design fault our menstrual cycles are. It could have been so simple. Go to shop, buy a baby. But no, we have to menstruate instead. It's rubbish.

I cooked meals for two families and dropped them round this weekend. It felt SO good to partake in some community activity and do something nice. I'm going to do more of that this week. For one family I made Jamie Oliver's 'Sausage and Cherry Tomato Bake' – my signature dish.

And for another, who are vegetarians, I roasted loads of veg and made a really good pasta sauce. I blended it all to look like tomato sauce, because their kid is fussy and that's his favourite. Everyone said they enjoyed the food, but I definitely want to expand my veggie repertoire to cook more exciting things than pasta for my vegetarian mates. I find it quite hard to be exciting without meat. Said the actress to the bishop.

I'm really scared about never having another buffet. Apparently 'the buffet' (my favourite meal) will be almost wiped out completely after Covid because people will be too afraid of them. IMAGINE hotels without buffet breakfasts? Pizza Hut without a salad bar? It's UNBEARABLE. I was OK with all this until I heard that, now I don't care if I never leave the house again. I might start an underground buffet movement, where we all gather in derelict mansion houses and eat from giant trays with our hands, because FUCK THIS.

On that note, I'm off to prepare a dinner spread of cocktail sausages and cheese on sticks for my family. ALL HAIL THE BUFFET.

I hope that you and yours are all OK.

Love Dawn x

24 May
Isolation Update – ALEXA, fix my womb

After another night of rolling around like a cat that had been hit by a car, courtesy of my uterus, I really could have done with a lie-in this morning. PLEASE can I just go to bed for a year? Instead, I was woken by Art, who was trying to be brilliant but not quite nailing it. He was asking Alexa to read to him, he was just doing it really loudly. 'ALEXA, PLAY "101 FACTS ABOUT DINOSAURS",' he yelled. To which Alexa yelled back 'HERE IS "101 FACTS ABOUT DINOSAURS".' To which I yelled, 'ALEXA, VOLUME FIVE.' But what did it matter, I was well and truly awake by then. So up I trudged into the kitchen to make them some cereal. Here we go again.

I am so pleased that my kids will never have to go through the trauma of period pain. Last night was so awful. If this was any other illness, I wouldn't feel like I have to get up and act normally, I would declare myself unwell and have Chris take over. And as much as he would if I asked, I don't do this because this isn't an illness, it's just how it bloody is. I know I've gone on about this before, but the way we women accept pain is crazy. Why, when I was up so much in the night, when I have taken way more painkillers than I should have, when I feel like I've been hit by a bloody truck, am I even pretending to be normal? I am either a trooper or pathetic, I'm not quite sure. I should be lying on my back screaming for crisps, demanding help and attention. Not cutting up a mango and spreading peanut butter on a bagel for someone else. It's ridiculous.

I had fried eggs on toast. Why isn't all food fried? It would just be so much better if it was, because then you wouldn't feel guilty when you eat it, because there wouldn't be any other options. Wouldn't that just be better?

As I am writing this, I can hear a massive house party a few doors down. I mean, for fuck's sake? I can't imagine they are wearing masks at this party. Some people really don't get it, do they? WATCH THE NEWS, YOU KNOBHEADS.

I don't need house parties, because I had a VERY exciting morning. I worked, then went to my local UPS store to pick up some printouts. Isn't that riveting? I know, I could barely contain myself. They even gave me a free folder for all my paperwork. I expressed a very over-the-top-level of gratitude, even using my arms at one point. It's amazing how one gesticulates when no one can see your face, isn't it?

We ran out of toilet paper and I went to three places to get some and they were all out. I eventually found some that is scented with lavender and I am almost positive it will give me thrush. WHY do I need my fanny to smell of lavender, to keep the moths out?

Do I tell you too much?

I'm pleased to say I have found some childcare and now have a few hours a day of help. It's a lovely lady called Fatima who is isolating at her house and just comes straight to us. Thank GOD. It's OBVIOUSLY game-changing, but the kids want to be with me anyway, and the time just flies. Still, it's one step closer to anything resembling normal, so I am very very happy and grateful about it. Finally, I get a few hours a day to work. We are really hoping the Governor (said in a broad Cockney accent with a cheeky wink) announces that small gatherings are allowed next week. I know that's coming in London soon, and New York has done it too. I really do feel like we could keep our life really tiny for ages. But we just need a couple of friends to do it with. Drinking alone has started to feel wrong.

Anyway, the kids are asleep so I'm going to get into bed and prepare myself for the onslaught of tonight's agony. You know, all entirely normal and everything. WTF.

NIGHT-NIGHT x

Love Dawn x

Earplugs, Eye Masks, Sleep Hats and Pills

At such a time of underlying stress, upheaval and anxiety, lockdown was a time in which we could have benefited from the best sleep of our lives. Instead, mine – mixed with grief – was a cocktail of crazy sleep patterns. And I'm sure I wasn't alone.

No matter what mood I went to bed in, my head would be full of terrifying visuals and dark, sad thoughts as soon as I tried to sleep. Around 12mg of melatonin, possibly a Benadryl and maybe more melatonin on the worse nights usually got me to sleep. It was there I'd meet those wild lockdown dreams that so many people have spoken about. For me they were epic: Hollywood blockbuster level action adventures. I think one night, The Rock even turned up. I'd often wake up with a start as I fell from a burning building, then need to take more melatonin to get me back to sleep again, otherwise I'd lie awake for hours and real life would feel like its own cinematic nightmare.

Lockdown has felt a world away from the good old snooze days of the past. I napped every afternoon before I had babies. I worked from home, writing, and at around 2 p.m. every day I'd become overwhelmed with yawns and would lie down, usually atop the covers, and fall asleep. This nap would last anywhere from twenty minutes to two hours, depending on what I had going on. If anyone tried to contact me in that time I would always get back to them saying, 'Sorry, was in a meeting' because there was something about being a grown-up who slept every afternoon that made me feel silly. I don't feel like that now though; when I hear about grown-ups napping, I think they are legit heroes. Why shouldn't grown-ups get as much sleep as they can? The pressure on us is huge. Sure, kids have to grow and stuff, but we have to THINK with our BRAINS.

When I got pregnant, the naps became even more important. I was in New York when I found out I was having Art. Chris was playing Lenny in *Of Mice and Men* on Broadway. He was excited to live a wild après theatre nocturnal life, but I couldn't keep my eyes open beyond 9 p.m. I'd wake up in the morning and know I had about two-hours of energy in the tank before I'd need to sleep again. As it turns out, growing a human really wipes you out. I slept and slept and slept. I'd generally pass out into the heaviest, most amazing snooze at around 1 p.m. and remain ensconced in my wild-but-fun pregnancy dreams until at least 4 p.m. I'd then walk around in a daze until it was acceptable for me to sleep again (usually around 9 p.m., if I wasn't meeting Chris after the show), and then I'd sleep through until 8 a.m. If I was meeting Chris, I'd just about manage a late-night meal around midnight. We'd often be with other people from the audience, and of course I couldn't drink or admit that I was up the duff, so it wasn't me at my best. I'd yawn my way through it and just make up lies about getting over food poisoning to explain why I wasn't chugging back cocktails. Then I'd get back to our place on all fours and crawl into bed like I'd just walked across a desert to get there. The next day I would sleep, and sleep, and sleep. God, it's almost worth having another baby, just for the naps. Not that it could be like that again, with the other two needing constant snacks and attention. And also, no more babies. Jesus. No fucking way.

As soon as I got Art home after he was born, I loved it. He was so easy. By easy, I don't mean *it* was easy. It was relentless. I was trying to run a business at the same time, and he screamed non-stop from 7–10 p.m. most nights. My nipples were red raw and I felt like my insides were going to fall out of my fanny. But for the most part, the first three months were my favourite part of all. I didn't get a full night's sleep, but I hadn't gone into motherhood to catch some zzz's. It was all OK, the night feeds were cute, the days were lazy. I could do newborns over and over again.

It's when my tiny baby started to move that the shit really hit the fan. No one warns you how much more work it is when they start to crawl. I missed my big squishy dollop who just lay there, unable to roll and fall on the floor, who I carried everywhere on my chest and who didn't knock over my wine. He went down from three naps a day to two, and then to one. During that nap I had so much to do that my own nap got ditched. And now, six years since my first pregnancy, that heavenly ritual of a daytime sleep is well and truly gone. I resent my children enormously for it. Isolation could have been so much more chill.

Throughout lockdown, I would imagine my alternative life. The me before the kids, before such sadness. Back then, if I woke in the night I'd reach for my computer and use the time to write. It didn't matter if I was up until 6 a.m., because I could then just sleep again until noon. I used to love getting up really early to work, my brain was always so active at about 7 a.m. I'd make coffee then get to it, bashing out thousands of words before 10 a.m. But those days are long gone. When you have kids, I believe you lose the two best times of the day to be creative: 6–10 a.m. and 4–8 p.m. The mornings are so intense with feeding them, dressing them, trying to get them out of the house, that there is no time for anything else. And their dinner, bath, bedtime routine means that those early evening hours are lost too. And then there's the anticipation of the morning stampede. Of course this means there's rarely such a thing as a lie-in, and why are they SO LOUD when they wake up? It's like they are playing a game of 'who-can-make-the-most-unnecessary-noise'.

The energy we're confronted with at 6 a.m. means I have to do whatever it takes to get to sleep while it's dark, and that means night times are stressful. The anxiety of not sleeping is often the thing that keeps me awake. Melatonin isn't addictive, but I get stressed at the thought of not having it. I think when you're a parent to young kids, you always have their safety in the back of your mind, and vigilance isn't exactly conducive to nestling down in bed. I can feel quite jolly and on top of things during the day, then as soon as I try to sleep my brain screams, 'ACTUALLY THINGS ARE NOT OK' and that's when I find myself eating cereal in the kitchen at 3 a.m.

I remember sleeping and sleeping and sleeping when Jane and I were teenagers and in our early twenties. We'd go and stay with our dad in Scotland for the summers, and the memory of him trying to wake us up in the afternoon is very vivid. I distinctly remember one day waking up and noticing that it was 3.30 p.m. Again, I recall a similar pattern when I was at drama school. I guess I did no exercise back then, and my diet was terrible, but sleeping until the afternoon is wild. I couldn't do that if I tried now. Even on the rare occasion Chris and I get a night off from the kids the very latest I can sleep until is around 8 a.m. Even if I'd only gone to bed a few hours earlier. Sleep as you get older is strange. You need less, but long for more. I'm lucky in that I can be quite functional on a small amount of sleep; it doesn't ruin me like it ruins some people. Which is why I was one of those freaks who enjoyed all the night feeds with my babies. But still, I'm through all that now and long for an eight-hour stretch with no interruptions. 'I feel like that might be a part of my near future,' I recently expressed to a friend. 'When the kids get just a little bit older, I'll get all the lovely sleep.' And she just said, 'Nope, menopause is worse for sleep than kids. So don't get too excited.'

Great. I wish I'd never bloody said it.

Lockdown could have been a lazy few months of word counts and naps. Alas, it was a frantic attempt to continue to achieve, on less sleep than normal and, by my own ready and willing admission, way too much weed and booze, which probably didn't help. But in all honesty, no matter how I complain, the mornings are my favourites. They generally start with Valentine creeping in and getting in with us, then Potato, then Art. Everyone is happy, everyone is cuddly. And no matter what kind of night I had, it always makes me happy because having a bed-full of men that I adore, is all I ever really wanted.

PIECE TWELVE

A Moment's Silence

26 May

Today was sad in so many ways. The video footage from the day before of the police officers in Minnesota murdering George Floyd in broad daylight was one of the most sickening things I have ever seen. A straight-up act of racist violence. It happens a lot in this FUCKING country, but my God, when it happens so brutally, in the middle of the day, surrounded by people, and totally unnecessarily, it's all the more agonising. It shows you how little regard so many police officers have for black lives and it's just so, so sad. They were fearlessly killing him in front of people. I hope they get the punishment they deserve. I couldn't believe what I was seeing when I saw that video. The blatancy of it, that poor man's voice, begging 'please, please'. He was saying he couldn't breathe, he called out for his mumma. It was so hard to watch, but so important that people do. For us to really understand what black people experience you have to witness it and acknowledge it – we don't have the right to turn away. But those images will never leave any of us. The only thing we can hope is that it is the catalyst for change. I am so sorry for George Floyd and his family. So sorry for every black person who has been brutalised, abused or murdered by police. To live in fear of the people who are supposed to protect you must be unbearable.

I've spent the past few years really listening to the conversation about racism. Until white people admit their part, and do the work to make things better, things will not change. I want to do better, and I have been reading and listening and doing my best to be an ally rather than another bystander. I'd urge you to be the same. To open your eyes and ears to what is happening, and to voice how it makes you feel. If you see an opportunity to do anything helpful, take it. Your efforts might feel small, but imagine if we all did what we could to speak up, call it out, and be a part of change rather than presuming it's down to someone else to make that happen. It's up to us all.

My heart goes out to George Floyd, his friends, family and his little girl. This should never have happened.

Love Dawn x

Let's Do Better

Around twenty years ago, in the big Sainsbury's at Dalston Junction, London, I needed to pay for some food. As I got in line a woman said, 'Excuse me,' and she sounded cross. I must have moved in front of her by mistake. I said, 'Oh, sorry, I didn't see you there.' And then she replied, 'You wouldn't have done that if I was white.'

WHOA!

I felt rage. How dare she accuse me of being racist because I didn't see her? I huffed about it, mortified by the accusation, feeling like all eyes were unfairly on me. I felt anger in that moment and carried it with me for years. The injustice of it. I'd just moved to London that week; I was intimidated by it all and didn't know where my life was going. As if I needed that on top of everything.

Oh, poor me.

Twenty years later and I have a very different perspective on what happened that day. The woman in Sainsbury's might have experienced multiple microaggressions just that morning. By the time I pushed past her in the supermarket, maybe she'd just had it with white people like me acting like she didn't exist. Maybe she had discovered that her white female colleague was being paid more than she was, despite the fact she works twice as hard. Maybe her employer had told her she couldn't wear her hair naturally at work, and maybe someone else had tried to touch it. Maybe she'd tried to speak up about a racist incident but was accused of being a bully and silenced, again. Maybe the night before she had watched yet another Hollywood film that failed to represent people with her skin colour. Maybe someone had shouted offensive racist slurs at her out of a car window. Maybe her kid is the only black kid in his school, and he is being bullied because of it. Maybe an old lady had clutched her handbag extra tight because they were alone in a lift together, and it made the woman feel horrible because she's never stolen a thing in her life. Maybe a white person at work had called her by the only other black person's name in the office. Maybe she had been in hospital and felt the level of care she received was less than the white woman in the bed next to her. Maybe she had read about another innocent black person in America being shot by the police. Each and every one of those scenarios is a real scenario that my black friends have told me about; the list, to be honest, goes on and on. I wish I could go back to that day in Dalston. Rather than huff away from the woman who thought I didn't see her, I'd look her in the eye and tell her I was sorry for getting in her way, rather than acting like she had done something wrong. That would have been the right thing to do.

At my workspace in LA, they use 'Slack' to communicate with us all. It's basically a kind of WhatsApp but with different 'channels' for different themes of chat. When the physical space shut down due to Covid, the digital community thrived. There was daily programming, meditations, stuff for kids and workshops. It was brilliant and the response from the members was always encouraging and enthusiastic. It's a group that celebrates diversity and is quite charged in terms of activism. Despite it being proud of its diversity, however, it remains a majority white-run organisation and that is something I know is being looked at. They focus a lot on the issue of race and dismantling inequality. They host 'racial affinity' workshops and do their best to inspire conversation despite how uncomfortable it might be. Most of the time it's a supportive, fun and fascinating group to be in. Until something goes wrong. One day, someone thought it would be funny to post a picture in the group of an old woman tying a noose. The caption read something like, 'How I'm feeling about marriage right now.' Or words to that effect. I never saw the post, it was taken down very quickly. What emerged next was a very official letter from the club explaining that the image of a noose symbolises historical racism and the lynching of black people by white people. The image was both offensive and triggering, and it was being taken very seriously. The person who posted it was being spoken to, and anyone who was hurt by the image had the club's full support. This was a 'zero-tolerance' response, and I admired it greatly. I messaged the person who would have been behind the letter, a friend of mine. I asked her if she was OK and said that I was sorry it had happened. I said the person who posted the image probably felt awful, and that I hoped they were OK because racism is an awful thing to be accused of. And this is where I finally understood what I (as a white person) keep doing. As my friend pointed out, we sympathise with the white person who caused the harm, rather than the black people who were hurt by their actions. It happens almost every time, and there I was doing it myself, despite my insistence that racism is a concept that applies to other people.

I do not consider myself a racist person, but 2020 has taught me that the word 'racism' isn't only about violence and verbal attacks. Sometimes an act of racism is very small, often totally missed by a white person but heard loud and clear by the person of colour to whom it was directed. This is the year that white people, no matter how un-racist they consider themselves to be, have had to examine even the smallest acts of discrimination that they project into the world every single day. Until white people, all white people, admit to their part in it, racism will never go away. If those of us who consider ourselves not to be racist only respond defensively when it's suggested that maybe we are, then nothing will ever change. With the incident at my workspace, I was confronted with the fact that my sympathy unconsciously falls with white people – this has been a personal lesson that I am taking on board, and I want that to change.

When I was growing up on Guernsey (it had a population of around 75,000 people), it was almost entirely white in its demographic. I didn't really know about racism because I never saw it. I never saw it because there were no black people around me for people to be racist towards, it's that simple. When I went to drama school in Liverpool, my eyes were opened to gayness, blackness, brownness, those who are able-bodied, those who aren't able-bodied, small town-ness, big town-ness and every kind of person. But it was still majority white. It wasn't something I questioned back then as it was what felt normal to me. I had a couple of black friends but never discussed race with them or had any real awareness that their experiences might have been different to mine. It was when I moved to Dalston in my early twenties and became nestled into a black community for the first time that I realised how sheltered I had been. I was beginning a career in TV. Most, if not all, of my colleagues were white. So much of the TV we were making involved white hosts and was aimed at a white audience. I lived in the heart of a black community, yet these people were not represented in the programmes I was making. I remember thinking this, but not saying it. When I started making documentaries and was on camera myself, I should have requested to have a more diverse crew. But I didn't. That was fifteen years ago, and people didn't talk about that kind of thing back then. I regret it enormously. It makes me as responsible. I should have requested diversity.

Last year, when I was doing the press tour for my novel *So Lucky*, I sat with my publicist and we talked about race. I had just read the book *So You Want to Talk About Race* by Ijeoma Oluo. Having become more involved with initiatives around diversity in my workspace in LA, and feeling less nervous to talk about it, I was realising more and more that the world I moved in was geared towards whiteness. It had also made me think about what my role in that was. I've never felt a responsibility as a writer to tell everybody's stories, but there should be more diversity in my novels. Why isn't there? It's something that bothers me a lot about my work, and now when I am reading books, I often find the whiteness irritating. Same with films and TV. If you haven't noticed, then look out for it. Look at how many black cast members there are in your favourite films and shows. Look out for the diversity on TV quiz shows, the characters in the books you read, voices on the radio. Once you start to notice, you can't un-notice it, and it's really got to change. In *So Lucky*, I left out physical descriptions of a few of the characters with the intention that they could be whoever the reader wanted them to be, but was that enough? I'm not sure it was. In another of my novels, *The Cows*, I had originally written the character Stella as a black woman. Only when I mentioned this to a black friend of mine, she told me to be careful. She warned me of tokenism, saying that unless I delved into the true experience of being black, I couldn't just have a black character. In a way she was right. *The Cows* deals with many themes, but racism isn't one of them. So, I created Stella as a white character. I became too nervous to write a black character, because I was afraid of getting it wrong. And so there it was, another novel by another white writer, full of whiteness and marketed towards white women. I regret it enormously.

I've had many uncomfortable moments in the past few years when discussing race but I am grateful for them all. When one of my black friends calls me out on something, it hurts, but I take it in. Another recent experience taught me something else; black people, especially black people here in America, are dealing with a level of continuous trauma that white girls like me will never understand. When I see the police, I feel safe. When they see the police, they feel afraid. Imagine that? I once came across an Instagram post by Snoop Dogg that read: 'If the police never did wrong people would trust them. Nobody ever made a song called "f*ck the fire department".' I thought it was well put, mildly amusing but also powerful. So I sent it to a black friend of mine, who has taught me more about racism than anyone in my life. I thought it would make her smile. It didn't. She responded by asking me kindly not to forward posts like that to her because we see these things through different eyes. I may see that as Snoop making a fair point, but to her it conjured images of violence and an institution killing people who look like her. It reminded her of the real threat that lives on the streets outside her apartment. It reminded her of hundreds of years of racism in the country she calls home. These lessons have been invaluable. I am grateful for them all. It's easy to get caught up in the social media version of anti-racism, but when you actually apply it to people who are living the experience, more sensitivity is needed. Not everyone lives the Instagram way. Most live the real way, and for them there is little appreciation for memes and quips.

I have insisted I am not racist for most of my life, but my whiteness and the whiteness I continue to prop up through my work, my social groups, the shows I watch, the books I read, the people I follow, the way I speak up, all needs examination.

After the murder of George Floyd, there were protests and riots quite literally on our doorstep, and it dragged my eyes fully open. At first, Chris and I were watching the Black Lives Matter protests on the local news and we kept commenting on how close it was. The protests were peaceful, until the cops showed up, creating a stand-off, and it all kicked off. There was violence and looting, and the crowds started to move. Soon helicopters started to circle our house. The sound of the protests got louder. People set fire to our trash cans and I was afraid the flames would catch and that we would need to escape. Chris and I put the kids to bed and I packed a bag, in case we needed to run. I was watching the news in our bedroom and could hear it on the street outside. It was unbelievable.

In the days that followed I walked down Melrose Avenue where the riots took place, and moments from my house there was a huge piece of graffiti saying the words, 'DADDY CHANGED THE WORLD.' It was referring to George Floyd. They were the words said by his six-year-old daughter after he was murdered by a policeman called Derek Chauvin, who pushed his knee into Floyd's neck for nearly nine minutes because he attempted to pay for something with a fake $20 bill. The devastating, but possibly hopeful, truth is that sweet little girl was right. There we were, all locked inside, only our TVs, radios and the Internet to relieve us from our own heads, and everybody had to listen for once. In the silence of lockdown, the streets were alive with the sounds of protests. The night the looters hit the shops outside my house, it was scary for a few reasons. There was fear, but also excitement. It felt like we could hear the world changing; all eyes and ears were on the news. Of course, no one with the right intentions wanted the violence, but the point of the protests came through loud and clear. I know it sounds strange, but it was an honour to be in the middle of it. In the weeks that followed, the peaceful protests went on and on. Chris got out there a number of times and I joined a couple myself. It was powerful and electrifying. People in cars handing out masks and water to those walking. A feeling of unity and activism for the greater good. Shops boarded up, but with beautiful and heart-warming graffiti all over the chipboard. The words 'BLACK LIVES MATTER' pasted loud and proud on every spare surface.

2020 saw the world shut down. Voices that had been screaming to be heard were finally the loudest we could hear. When we re-emerge from the fear and anxiety that the virus has instilled into us all, maybe more people than ever will have the chance to feel safe.

New Beginnings

4 June
Isolation Update – Nappy off, nappy face

You know when the world outside is really scary, so you find an article about killer mosquitoes that live in your city just to chill you out?

I DO.

Actually I lied, outside isn't that scary any more. Not now the rioting has stopped. Protests are still going on, but they are peaceful and wonderful. It was calm on Melrose Avenue just now. Minus all the men with machine guns (they deployed the National Guard to keep us all in check). Business owners were taking down boards and sorting through what was left of their stock. Everyone was being kind and chatty and there was a real feeling of community. I saw a few restaurants opening, and the graffiti on the walls denoted a feeling of support and hope. This area took a real battering, but something tells me it will come back stronger than ever.

It's weird that the riots are over. It was so consuming, at times we even totally forgot about the pandemic. It was like the world had moved on, we had something new to worry about. It's strange to say it, but lockdown sort of feels safe and normal after all that. Who'd have thought the quiet of isolation could feel so comforting?

Everyone is wondering if there will be a huge spike in corona cases after the protests, but what if there isn't? Do we then presume the government has been lying to us? I heard from one family that their granddad had died in hospital a few weeks ago. The hospital wrote that the cause of death was

Covid-19, even though it wasn't. They did it because hospitals get a payout for every Covid case. Does that mean less people than reported have died of it, so the hospitals can make money??

CAN YOU IMAGINE? I could believe that for America, but that doesn't make sense for the UK, for example, where there is an NHS. I don't know who to believe. WHO SHOULD I BELIEVE, GUYS??

Oh, back to the trials and tribulations of us potty training Valentine for a moment. I am pleased to announce that my nappy days are done. Both kids are out of them day and night now. WHAT a moment for us as parents, and a sigh of relief for the landfills. Delighted not to be contributing to their breaking points any more. And more delighted not to be constantly scraping shit off a small person's legs.

SMALL VICTORIES.

Love Dawn x

9 June
Isolation Update – That's it, baby, kick the shit out of the problem

Earlier on I found Art outside punching the air.

'Art, what are you doing?'

'I'm beating up Isolation.'

He's gonna be OK, right?

Valentine has refused to eat dinner for over a week now. I'm not worried about him, he eats all day and is absolutely massive. It's just annoying because I then eat what he doesn't eat, and I am also getting absolutely massive.

I realised today that we have been in this for three months now. What toll is that having on us all? The kids seem OK, but I know Art gets really sad about missing his friends. I remain so grateful this happened to my kids while they are this age. WHEN this is over, they will fit back into normal life easily, I know it. And thank God they have each other; Art and Valentine's friendship has been beautiful to watch. Sweet boys. I'm excited for them as brothers; a lifetime of having each other. Lockdown has set that relationship in stone, it's very cute. And for Chris and me, precious time with them that we will look back on with so much love, as parents generally do when referring back to the younger years. It's amazing how the memories of the tantrums and the poo-stained furniture leave you over time, but they do.

The thing that worries me the most in the repercussions of this, even more so than the social aspects because the kids have actually had a lot of fun, is that they will end up being total germophobes. The thought of that makes me so sad. If they do go back to school in the autumn, the level of hygiene pushed on them will be insane, and rightfully so, but also, what's THAT going to do to them long-term? They haven't really experienced that at home. Sure, we make them wash their hands if they go to the park, and I spray them with anti-bac if we go out, but at home they are as feral as kids are supposed to be. At school, they will have to wear masks all the time, they won't be allowed to breathe near each other, playing where they touch, there'll be constant hand washing, Perspex sheets between them. No contact with anyone. I hope that doesn't have any long-term effects like them being unable to relax in crowds or get all weird and tense when people try to get close to them. I can't bear the idea of that. Hopefully the way we are at home rubs off on them more than the sterile world they will enter into at school. I'll stop cleaning completely, just to make sure they are exposed to some germs. Kids NEED germs. *Puts hoover away and lies down.

I've been trying to drink pretentious tea at teatime, instead of wine. All that happens is I drink the tea and then drink the wine. But at least I drank the tea, right?

I found a box of tangerine tea today. It said 'POSITIVE ENERGY' on it. I put four bags in one cup and was still in a bad mood by the time I finished it. What a waste of water.

HOLD TIGHT FOR MY BIG NEWS.

Tonight, I am doing something dramatically different with a rib-eye steak. I am marinating it in soy sauce, garlic, honey and garlic. I will fry it and slice it, and lay it lovingly upon brown rice, and serve with a side of Teriyaki carrots. I'm scared. I love the way I do steak, but I became overwhelmed with the need to push the proverbial boat out, and here we are.

Not that it really matters what I cook, I'm never hungry by dinner time because I eat constantly all day.

Anyway, I better go and make it.

Before another day begins.

Love Dawn x

12 June
Isolation Update – Re-emerge the same but better

Guys, it's been a nice week. Sweltering, but nice. I got work done so I don't feel like I'm staring at an intimidating blank page any more. The kids are happy, and my clothes fit again. RESULT. I didn't have a single margarita, not a single one. But it's 2 p.m. on a Friday afternoon right now, and I am counting the minutes until 4 p.m., because I just nominated that as the time I will have my first cocktail of the weekend. Oh yes. Let the good limes squeeze.

I worked hard this week. I found some focus. This is great because, if I'm honest, a couple of weeks ago I didn't know how I'd focus. The world outside was teaching us a lesson after the death of George Floyd, and I heard it loud and clear. The work now happens within these four walls: in what I watch, in what I read, in what I write. Everything is changing. I am determined not to see the protests, the riots, the killing of so many innocent black people as a moment in time. It is to come with us all into the future, and we have to make continuous and long-lasting effort to do better. I started listening to *White Fragility* on audiobook by Robin Diangelo. It's a wake-up call for realising things about yourself that maybe you didn't want to see. I recommend it to you all, if you are white, and you don't understand what it means to have the white privilege that you absolutely have. It's OK to realise things about yourself that make you uncomfortable, because that can help you do a better job of being a part of the solution. Read it, it's worth your time. When isolation is over, let's materialise as a better version of what we were before.

Um . . . what else? Is it 4 p.m. yet?

Damn it. Why does time go so slowly?

I am cooking Jamie Oliver's 'Sweet Sausage and Cherry Tomato Bake' tonight. A real classic that I've told you about before. I'm going to bake sweet potatoes to go with it and serve with a rocket and parmesan salad. That is if I don't get wasted by 7 p.m., and just order pizza. Of course, you will be the first to know.

Sending you all the love in the world.

Dawn x

30 June
Isolation Update – BOOBS BOOBS BOOBS

In a minute I am going for my annual breast check. It's been in the diary for two months, but they just called me to say the mammogram machine isn't working, so do I want to reschedule, or just have the ultrasound? I said just the ultrasound is fine. I woke up at 4 a.m. feeling really nervous about it. If I was my mother, I'd have died of breast cancer six years ago. I wonder if today will be the day I am told I have it too.

I'd be lying if I said there isn't a part of me that wants to be told I have early signs of breast cancer so I can take action. I don't have the BRACA gene, so until a diagnosis there is no point in doing anything. But at even the hint of something being wrong, I think I'd just get a double mastectomy and be done with this thing that hangs over me. I'd get lovely new perky boobs and would finally be able to wear strapless dresses without horrible bras that slide down my body. I try to focus on the positives before every check-up, because maybe some new boobies wouldn't be so bad.

OK, it's time to go.

UPDATE: I just got back. ALL CLEAR. Thank goodness. I like the ultrasound because it's a better view of the inside of my boobs. I need it because I have very dense breast tissue (they don't feel very dense) and they can't quite see what's going on with the mammogram, so the machine being broken really wasn't a problem. As the lovely doctor splodged KY jelly all over my boobs, then pressed the camera thingy on to me (I hate it when she goes over my nipples, it makes me feel all weird) she told me to look at the screen. 'It all looks perfect,' she kept saying, to my relief.

'What does cancer look like?' I asked.

'It looks like a storm,' she said, and I felt the room go cold.

A storm. What a description, I can't stop thinking about it. In that vein, there wasn't a breeze in sight, a strangely relaxing thing to look at, considering it was the inside of my breast. Not even the hint of a storm on the horizon. I feel very, very grateful. This time next year I will be hoping there are no dark clouds.

My health has always been of great concern, simply because my mum died of breast cancer at thirty-six. It means doctors have always made serious faces at me, and the words 'check your breasts' have been said more times than I can count.

There are women who get breast cancer out of nowhere, no family history, no reason to expect it. I consider myself lucky that I am able to be so 'on it'. As much as I get nervous before I go for a check-up, I know I'm in a really good position to fight it because of the level of vigilance I have.

In other news, we might be able to get into our new house in a matter of weeks! I can't believe the day will actually come. To think we started this year and thought that would be the biggest thing that would happen. People always say that moving house is the most stressful thing you can do. Add losing someone you love, a global pandemic and riots on your doorstep into the mix and wow, it's been quite the few months. But here we are, facing so much good stuff too. We are healthy, we have each other, and I cannot wait to get my family settled into our new home. We're very lucky, and I am grateful for it all.

I am going to make a cup of tea and then have a stronger drink to celebrate me and my healthy boobs.

Love Dawn x

1 July
Isolation update – A Fish called Hippo

Today, my baby Valentine turned three. To think this time three years ago I had just done THAT. Val's birth was a brilliant experience. Quick, and on the bed at home. BOOYA.

What an absolute joy having Valentine has been. Such an amazing kid. We got him loads of sharks and dinosaurs for his birthday so he is happy. It really is all he wants in the world. We are about to have a little cake and some pizza. Gorgeous!

I love my family. I couldn't have done isolation with anyone else.

OH, and we are about to present the fish. Valentine's obsession with sea creatures is life-long. To have his very own yellow (fave colour) fish, might blow the head clean off him. Either that or he will eat it. Which is also likely.

UPDATE: We presented the fish, the boys LOVE him and so do I. He currently lives on my desk and I have no plans to move him. He comes over to say hi when I sit down. He loves blood worms though, gross. Anyway, he's so cute and his name . . . courtesy of Valentine and his random brain: Hippo.

That's right, we have a fish called Hippo. So that's happening. Welcome to the family, little man, you are very welcome and we are home A LOT.

Love Dawn x

9 July
Isolation Update – We un-isolated and isolated somewhere else

We just got back home from a trip to Ojai for three days. It's about an hour and a half away and heaven on earth.

Three days was all it took, I am a new person. We did something we have never done before and took childcare with us, so we split the days with Fatima – the kids just love Fatima, so we were really happy she could come on holiday with us too. It was THE DREAM: I went for walks alone. I swam alone. We got drunk every night then watched *Hamilton* on mushrooms (recommended). We ate loads. We walked in an orange grove with the kids every morning and picked oranges off the trees to eat as we looked out for snakes. We swam as the sun went down.

WE GOT OUT OF OUR HOUSE AND IT WAS INCREDIBLE.

Three days. It's all you need. One thing I noticed was how quickly I was able to chill. Usually I get there (it's a friend's house, we go there often but he wasn't there this time) and by about halfway through the second day, I maybe start to relax. Maybe. Coming from work/life pressure. Busy busy. So many to-do lists, etc. etc., means I'm usually too hyped up to calm down. I am not the kind of person that can just turn life off and chill (you may have noticed). Mini-breaks during lockdown are different. You get there already slow. I arrived at the house, put on my swimsuit, poured a drink and I was 💯 in holiday mode. Even though I worked all day Tuesday, I was still in holiday mode. I like working. I don't mind doing it on holiday, especially next to a pool with a drink.

This trip was the first time I have had a real moment to think about Caroline. I mean, I'm never not thinking about her, but this was proper thinking. With space. Not at home. Out in the open. Happy thoughts. Sad thoughts. I could finally hear them all. I went for one walk and found myself laughing. Actually laughing out loud at my memories of us together.

I was surrounded by mountains and beauty, and I really felt lucky because I got to have Caroline in my life at all. I have so many memories, all of them good. I get to keep those and take them with me. My memories make me smile at mountains and look up to the sky, take a deep breath and know that my life is richer because of the fun we had. How can I only be sad? That would be stupid. I realised that on holiday. Death is so awful. So final. So disrupting. But it's also there to remind us to keep living. When you've gone, all that matters is what you did. So you might as well do it well. Caroline was excellent at life. I'm going to do my best to be excellent at mine. That means laughing more than crying, and feeling lucky for what we had rather than feeling robbed of what could have been.

I hope this feeling lasts. It's better.

We stopped off at the beach on the way home and the kids were so happy. Must do more beach. It's nice to be home, especially as this will only be our home for the next few weeks. We'll have to cherish every moment. So many good times in this house, there is still time to have some more.

I did miss Hippo though. He seems cross I left him. Next time, the fish comes. Maybe even Lilu too, if she promises not to piss on anything.

Love Dawn x

Epilogue

Dear 2020,

I think a lot about the things I would like to forget. I'd like to forget the night my mum died, and the morning Caroline died. I'd like to forget some bad experiences with guys, some fights with friends and a few with Chris. I have some terrible memories of being a young girl. I'd happily remove a few instances where I have behaved badly and upset people, and others where people have said things that have hurt my ego. There are memories that I wish would go away, because they don't serve me well and just trouble me (mostly when I have a hangover or can't sleep). And then there's 2020: we could just forget entirely about it and start afresh in 2021 when everything is going to be perfect, right? RIGHT?

But forgetting things won't get me anywhere. Caroline dying gave me compassion for those who have lost people through suicide. My mother's death means I understand what childhood trauma can do. My fights with my husband have forced me to listen, and any mean things I have said have left me guilt-ridden and sorry. My bad experiences with men have made me an excellent mother to boys. My fall-outs with friends have made me a better friend to the ones I keep. I've learned from them all. All pain is worth it. All mistakes make us better, all fear more understanding, all love more open. Every experience we have prepares us for something else down the road. It's all just life, and whoever said that was going to be easy? No one did, and if they did, they were likely lying or exceptionally boring.

So what have I learned about myself in lockdown? I've always wondered what my other life could look like. The one where I'm single with no kids, where I live in a nice flat in London, alone, with a couple of cats, writing novels in my bed. I've often wondered if that life would have suited me more – if I'm just trying on a version of the person I am now, rather than really being her. But lockdown has taught me that I am *so* her. So fully and completely, with dedication and every inch of my soul. I am a wife and a mother and this life is the one I want to be in, no doubt. I want to be friends with the school mums. I want to cheer my kids on when they play sport (if they are ever allowed to play sport again). I want to make EXCELLENT cupcakes for bake sale and costumes for Halloween. I can be that woman. I AM that woman. I don't have to be good at pretending, I *am* good at this. I love being at home, I LOVE my friends, I adore my job. I feel very deeply and I am spiritual as hell (remember those crystals?) as long as people don't bang on about it too much. I know I can survive with a few close people, rather than seeking the approval of thousands, and that is a huge and wonderful relief. I know myself a little better than I did before, and I like myself more for the knowledge.

Putting a positive spin on things isn't easy, though. I wasn't really raised that way. When I was growing up, conversations at our dinner table would happily lean into the terrible. It wasn't that we were a sad family, quite the opposite. But as a collective, we didn't hold back from sharing the bad things that happened over the course of a day, as well as the good. I think it's probably quite British. I actually (also quite British) like being that way. Never enjoying anyone else's pain, but always happy to discuss it. Just yesterday, Chris came into the office to say, 'hi' to me and I immediately said that I was worried about my friend's new house in case there were more fires in California. 'Wow,' he said. 'Your brain really goes to a dark place, doesn't it?' And I just said, 'Yeah. Yeah, it really does.' It always has. I'm kind of used to it.

Irish people tend to focus on the positives. Gratefulness is a big part of the culture, or so it seems. If a conversation starts heading too far down a depressing road, someone is sure to bring it back. I found this quite hard when I was first around my in-laws, always feeling like the Debbie Downer at the table who wanted to get into the nitty-gritty of any recent tragedies, only to be stopped when things (as far as I was concerned) were getting really juicy. I've had to learn to find a middle ground. But isolation has been a challenge for me: the grief, the fear, the loneliness, the distance from the people I love, the political unrest and anxiety, the terrifying death rates, the never-being-able-to-leave-the-house, the relentless childcare and many sleepless nights. I had to learn not to wallow in it all, it wouldn't have been fair on my family. If I had succumbed completely to grief, my kids' memories of this time would be traumatic. I wanted it to be a period of fun family time, where they had way more sugar than usual, went to bed late, and had me and Chris mostly to themselves for months on end. They have no idea how sad I have been, but I protected it from them because I wanted to. I did that, and I did it well while taking care of myself too. I'm proud of myself for that. I did good. When the world goes mad, you either go mad with it, or focus on the things that are OK. And there were loads of things that were OK. More than OK. My house is lovely, my kids are awesome and I love my husband so much. That was what got me through. The life that we have built. It was strong – not even Covid-19 could knock it down. And luckily, for now, there is no storm.

As I look back over the last few months of a year that has changed us all, I can see how so much of life happens when nothing is really happening. I'd go so far as to say that the smaller your life gets, the more room there is for your emotions to grow. Without the distraction of normal life, I have cried, hurt and loved harder than I ever thought possible. I've been able to spend time with myself, my kids, my husband and my dog and my cat and now my fish. And I've realised that the way I feel when I am with them is me at my very best. I don't know what the future holds, 2020 has taught me not to presume anything, but what I do know is that another chapter will begin. Soon, we'll close the door on our old house where we lived as newlyweds. The first place we brought Art home to, the house where we conceived and then I gave birth to Valentine. The house where we hosted more parties than we can remember. The house that friends lived in while we were away, where babies, not just our own, took their first steps in. A house full of so many memories, eight years of love and a million other emotions from laughing to screaming, shouting and a hell of a lot of crying in cupboards. It's a house of 40 billion cockroaches. A million meals cooked and an infinity of margaritas drunk. Many a weed gummy consumed and some seriously excellent kaftans worn. This house was the last place where I saw Caroline, on 22 October 2019. It's where I was when I received that call. It's seen me at my most powerful as I brought life into this world, and my absolute weakest as I saw it disappear. And now we are moving. Just me and my favourite people. To a new house. A new start. There are no memories there, only the ones we decide to take with us.

I'm going to take them all.

Love Dawn x

A Note from Dawn

At the start of the year I was looking for ways to feel a bit more secure in my work. I've been writing full-time for the best part of a decade, but even so, a regular income from doing what I do has always felt like a pipe dream. When *Glamour* magazine stopped its monthly print edition at the end of 2017, I lost my regular column and I missed writing in that way. Columns are personal and fun, a great outlet for thoughts. I had my books and Instagram to express myself but there was nowhere to put anything longer and more intimate. The idea of blogging for no financial return didn't work for me. I see the Internet as a place where artists largely work for free, and at forty-one I was done with that. I needed a secure and regular income, but I also didn't want to be beholden to brands. That's when I discovered Patreon. It's a slightly terrifying concept whereby people subscribe online for a fee and I write for them. I set up my account, feeling like a real dick for even trying, but wondered if anyone might be up for it. I kept the price low: $4 for all. There's a tier system on Patreon where subscribers can access more or less content depending on how much they pay. I felt weird about that, so kept the fee low for everyone. My goal was for more people to pay less, rather than have a few people paying more. I am no businesswoman, but that felt like a good plan. I set up the page and posted about it on Instagram, then went and hid in a cupboard because I was so scared.

When I emerged, I had a few hundred subscribers. This was enough to justify my time. So, I started to write. Every time I posted that I had written something on Instagram, lots of people got mad at me asking why they should pay 'for my crap'. Or telling me I didn't need the money so why was I charging for my work? This reaffirmed that I was doing exactly the right thing. I saw it more like, how had I NOT been charging for my work for so long? I quickly realised that as long as I delivered on the content, the transaction was a fair exchange. My promise was a blog post a week plus lots of other bits and bobs – a podcast, occasional videos, giveaways and more, but mostly words. Lots and lots of words. As more and more readers signed up, all that worried me was that I wouldn't have enough to say.

For this reason, and this reason alone, I would like to thank 2020 for the unrivalled amount of material it has offered me. When lockdown started and I had no childcare, I couldn't write the novel I was about to start – my head was miles away from that focus. But I was feeling feelings I'd never felt, living a life I'd never lived. I had so much to say and, with the Patreon platform, I had somewhere to say it. So I wrote and wrote and wrote. When the kids were in bed, I wrote. When they were watching TV, I smashed out an 'Isolation Update.' While I watched them eat, I made notes on my phone. It became an obsession. I spilled some milk, my subscribers needed to know about it. I wrote about everything from parenting and cooking to grief and the TV we watched.

The tiny aspects of life became each day's top story. And this is how *Life in Pieces* had its early origins.

The Patreon community grew and grew and became a place of solace for me. After Caroline died, I found the Internet a terrifying place to be. I didn't want to put myself out there if I was only going to be met with negativity. So I created my own little corner of it, where I could be entirely myself and write for a group of people who all wanted to be there. It's SO nice. I do hope you've enjoyed the book that has come out of it. And if you are so inclined, feel free to sign up to my blog on Patreon. It's fun, and as you will see, I work very, very hard for it.

Acknowledgements

I'm going to keep these brief as I mentioned so many of the people I love in the book itself, and hopefully that shows my appreciation. But on top of that . . .

Thanks so much to everyone at HarperCollins for making this book happen. I have no idea how we turned that blog into a book, but we did. Specific shout-outs to Charlotte and Kimberley for being the dream editing team. Liz for getting the book out there, and Claire for the cover.

Thanks to my agent, Adrian Sington, who has been there from the start and who I adore so much.

Thanks to Josie, for so many things. I couldn't have done those weeks without you. I love you.

Thanks to each and every one of my Patreon subscribers. I LOVE writing the blog for you, and when I look back on isolation, if it ever ends, you will be a massive part of it. Thank you for the support and I will continue to keep my fingers fingering for you.

And mostly, thanks to Chris, Art, Valentine, Lilu, Potato and Hippo. My isolation team. I couldn't have done it with anyone else. Team O'. The best. I'm very lucky that you're mine.